C000262445

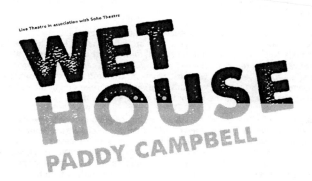

Live Theatre in association with Soho Theatre

WET HOUSE

PADDY CAMPBELL

Wet House was first performed at Live Theatre, Newcastle as part of the company's 40th birthday year on Thursday 19 September 2013.

WEDNESDAY 17 SEPTEMBER TO SATURDAY 11 OCTOBER 2014
Live Theatre, Newcastle

TUESDAY 14 TO SATURDAY 18 OCTOBER 2014
Hull Truck Theatre, Hull

WEDNESDAY 22 OCTOBER TO SUNDAY 16 NOVEMBER 2014
Soho Theatre, London

SERVING THEATRE

S F

SINCE 1830

SAMUELFRENCH-LONDON.CO.UK
SAMUELFRENCH.COM

A Word from the Writer

A few years back I got a job working in a wet house, a homeless hostel for alcoholics where they could drink round the clock. The idea was that they were in a secure environment, to reduce the social problems caused by homeless alcoholics on the streets. In reality it housed anyone, people the system struggled to place – drug addicts, the mentally ill, sex offenders and young care leavers. At the time you wouldn't have got me anywhere near a theatre, let alone sit down to write a play.

So no lifelong love affair with the stage. As a child, I'd been taken to see my Dad act in plays in the Lyric Theatre in Belfast. Unfortunately, I was hyperactive in a time before Ritalin and couldn't sit still for longer than five minutes. My mother was demented. School plays were another lost cause. The drama teacher soon realised that it was best, whatever the production, to shoehorn in a Tarzan character. This way, he could send me to the other end of the hall to swing on the ropes while the rest of them rehearsed the play.

Having dabbled with a bit of short story writing, I signed up to a playwriting course at Live Theatre. For a change, I didn't appear to be bottom of the class and no one threw a chalk duster at me for being obscene. I joined Live's writers group and entered a short play in a competition. It came second, which spurred me on to try and do greater things. By the time I was half way through the next one, writing plays had become all consuming. I'd studied sculpture at university but hadn't exactly set the art world alight since graduating. Here was something which satisfied my artistic soul and at the same time I could cram full of dysfunctional nut jobs and squalid knob gags. A win win situation if ever there was one.

Over the last few years, I've been fortunate to have had a number of short plays produced by Live Theatre, serving as a kind of apprenticeship for writing my first full length play, which I knew I had to set in a wet house. I had a good setting, but it was the other bits, like a plot, which were proving complicated. Now, I'm certainly not saying that everyone who works in a wet house are latent inebriates themselves, but in some cases, certainly mine, prolonged periods of time spent around self-destructive people brought out some nihilistic tendencies. I couldn't tell you if this is a predisposition or a direct influence of the environment (probably a combination of both), but I decided that a play which charted this, let's call it personal and spiritual decay, would be a good place to start. Day to day life in the wet house was horrific and hysterical in equal measures. Humour, often the blackest black, was used as a coping mechanism by residents and staff alike, I aimed to reflect this in the play.

I am thrilled that Live Theatre has brought *Wet House* back after producing it for their 40th birthday. It felt like the first run was over in a flash. I would particularly like to thank Max Roberts for both championing and directing the play. The cast have been utterly fearless and honest in telling this story and it is a privilege to have such talented actors performing your words. They have also helped make some great improvements to the script. I'd like to express my heartfelt gratitude to everyone at Live Theatre who has supported my writing over the years, in particular Gez Casey who has been instrumental in the development of this play.

Paddy Campbell

A word from the director

What struck me most starkly about *Wet House* on reading the play for the first time was that it contained a vivid sense of authenticity.

The play is based on Paddy's experiences in the care industry when he initially graduated from Northumbria University about 6 years ago. Whilst it's obviously fiction, he's managed to capture a credulity of a world that many of us can only imagine.

Paddy's play presents an uncomfortable reality inherent in contemporary society that isn't always acknowledged or examined.

Whilst the subject matter is challenging and at times the action is quite shocking, Paddy's brilliant sense of humour and deft skill in writing authentic dialogue makes the harrowing and tragic content of the play completely accessible.

That as a young writer he has chosen to present a serious, political subject, skilfully employing comic, tragic and daring theatricality is a testament to his talent, maturity and potential. I really hope audiences who come to the show can say that they have seen the arrival of yet another outstanding talent to emerge from Live Theatre's long list of outstanding north east writers.

Max Roberts
Artistic Director, Live Theatre

CAST (in order of appearance)

Helen	Jackie Lye
Mike	Chris Connel
Andy	Riley Jones
Dinger	Joe Caffrey
Kerry	Eva Quinn
Spencer	Simon Roberts

CREATIVE & PRODUCTION TEAM

Writer	Paddy Campbell
Director	Max Roberts
Designer	Gary McCann
Lighting Designer	Drummond Orr
Sound Designer	Dave Flynn
Video Designer	Paul Aziz
Fight Director	Paul Benzig
Production Manager	Drummond Orr
Stage Manager	Adam Johnston
Deputy Stage Manager	Heather Robertson
Costume Supervisor	Lou Duffy
Assistant Director	Anna Ryder
Assistant Designer	Florence Hazard
Casting	Sooki McShane CDG
Casting	Lucy Jenkins CDG

FOR LIVE THEATRE

Creative Producer	Graeme Thompson
Technical Manager	Dave Flynn
Technicians	Hannah Gregory & Sam Stewart
Technical Apprentice	Craig Spence

FOR ASSISTED PERFORMANCES

British Sign Language	Caroline Ryan
Captioning	Christopher Phillips
Audio Description & Touch Tour	Michael Davies

CAST

JACKIE LYE Helen

Jackie trained at Central School of Speech and Drama and has worked extensively in theatre and television ever since.

Theatre credits include: *Julie & Paul* (LOST Festival), *Smack Family Robinson* (Fruit), *Christmas Office Party, A Kick In The Baubles, Going Dutch, Julius Caesar* and *Oh Baby* (Hull Truck Theatre), *Cooking with Elvis* (Hull Truck Theatre and tour), *I Want That Hair* (York Theatre Royal), *Inglorious Technicolour* (Stephen Joseph Theatre), *Caucasian Chalk Circle* (Oxford Playhouse/Young Vic), *Strippers* (Duncan C Weldon Ltd, tour and West End) and *Turcaret* (Gate Theatre).

Television credits include: *Brush Strokes* (6 series), *Doctors* and *Casualty* (BBC), *The Bill* and *London's Burning* (ITV) and 4 series of *Harry's Mad* (Central).

CHRIS CONNEL Mike

Theatre credits include: *The Pitmen Painters* (Live Theatre/National Theatre, Broadway and national tour), *Close the Coalhouse Door* (Northern Stage/Live Theatre and national tour), *The Prize, Nativities, Cooking with Elvis* and *Toast* (Live Theatre), *Shooting the Legend* (Theatre Royal Newcastle), *Cooking with Elvis, Bouncers, Studs, Up On Roof* and *A Kick In The Baubles* (Hull Truck Theatre), *Bouncers* (Ambassadors Theatre Group), *Black on White Shorts* (Paines Plough/Live Theatre), *And a Nightingale Sang* (Cheltenham Everyman), *The Steal and Men, Women, Inspectors and Dogs* (Theatre Royal York/Cloud Nine), *Peer Gynt* (Three Over Eden Theatre Company), *Cuddys Miles* (Customs House) and *Unreal* (Cloud Nine).

Film and television credits include: *Goal* (Icon) and *Purely Belter* (Mumbo Jumbo/ Film Four), *Emmerdale, Heartbeat* and *How We Used To Live* (YTV), *The Round Tower* (Festival Films), *Badger, Crocodile Shoes* and *Breeze Block* (BBC), *George Gently* (Company Pictures), *The Bill* (ITV), *Byker Grove* (BBC/Zenith), *Quayside* (Zenith/ Tyne Tees), *King Leek* and *Steel River Blues* (Granada Television), *Finney* (Zenith/ Carlton), *The Block* (Channel 4), *Take Me* (Scottish TV/Coastal Productions), *Lawless* (Company/ITV) and *Nelson's Navy* (October Films for Channel 4).

Radio credits include: *Torchbearers, The Gallery, The Pitmen Painters, Poor Clare, The Song Thief, A Man's World* and *Skellig* (BBC).

RILEY JONES Andy

Riley trained at Northumbria University, Newcastle.

Theatre credits include: *Harold Larwood* by Lee Hall & Simon Beaufoy, *Rocket Man* and *For The End of Time* by Lee Hall (rehearsed readings), *Cooking with Elvis, Islanders* (rehearsed reading) and *Short Cuts* (Live Theatre), *The Pitmen Painters* (Live Theatre/National Theatre/Bill Kenwright Ltd, national tour), *Close the Coalhouse Door* (Gala Theatre), *A Bit of Respect* (Operating Theatre) and credits with Theatre And and Bruvvers Theatre Company.

Television credits include: *Vera* (ITV), *Wolfblood* and *United* (BBC).

JOE CAFFREY Dinger

Joe trained at LAMDA. He won Performer of the Year at the 2013 Journal Culture Awards for his roles in the Live Theatre productions *Wet House, Cooking with Elvis* and *The Pitmen Painters*.

Theatre credits include: *Harold Larwood* by Lee Hall & Simon Beaufoy and *For The End of Time* by Lee Hall (rehearsed readings) and *Cooking with Elvis* (Live Theatre), *The Pitmen Painters* (Live Theatre/National Theatre/Bill Kenwright Ltd, West End and national tour), *A Walk On Part* (Live Theatre/Soho Theatre, West End), *Much Ado About Nothing, The Globe Mysteries, Loves Labours Lost* and *We the People* (Shakespeare's Globe Theatre), *Billy Elliot The Musical* (Victoria Palace Theatre), *Keepers of the Flame* (RSC/Live Theatre), *Black and White Shorts* (Live Theatre/Paines Plough), *Studs* (Hull Truck Theatre) and *Cooking with Elvis* (Live Theatre West End/national tour).

Television and film credits include: *Wolfblood, Clay, Doctors, Holby City, Attachments, Badger, Hetty Wainthrope Investigates, Spender* and *Byker Grove* (BBC), *Heartbeat, The Bill, Distant Shores, Colour Blind – Catherine Cookson, Quayside, Waiters, The Last Musketeer, Ain't Misbehavin* and *Soldier, Soldier* (ITV), *In Fading Light* (Amber Films), *The One and Only* (Assassin Films) and *Bridget Jones – The Edge of Reason* (Working Title Films).

EVA QUINN Kerry

Eva trained at East 15 Acting School, London.

Theatre credits include: *Rocket Man* by Lee Hall (rehearsed reading), *Between The Lines, First Draft, Lion, Home Help* and *Short Cuts* (Live Theatre), *Bunker Blues* (Curious Monkey), *Geronimo* (Company TSU), *Untitled* (Nabokov) and *Rattle & Roll* (Open Clasp Theatre Company).

Film and television credits include: *Lost Girl* (Writer's Block North East), *You Locked The Door* (Meercat Films), *Sleepworking* (Northern Film & Media), *Celluloid Dreams* (Scala Productions/2nd Floor Productions), *George Gently* (BBC) and *Vera* (ITV).

SIMON ROBERTS Spencer

Simon trained at LAMDA and is making his Live Theatre debut.

Theatre credits include: *Another Country* (Queen's Theatre), *The Life and Adventures of Nicholas Nickleby parts 1 and 2* (Gielgud Theatre/Princess of Wales Theatre Toronto/Chichester Festival Theatre), *Volpone* (Theatre Babel), *Not About Heroes* (Byre Theatre), *The Tempest* (Liverpool Playhouse), *Smoking with Lulu* (Citizens Theatre), *The Taming of the Shrew* (Royal Exchange Theatre), *King Lear* (Young Vic and Japan), *As You Like It* (Old Vic), *Amphitryon* (Gate Theatre), *A Flea in Her Ear* (Theatr Clwyd), *The Rivals* (Nottingham Playhouse), *Midsummer Night's Dream* (Renaissance Theatre World Tour), *The Park* (Sheffield Crucible), *Untold Stories* and *Cat on a Hot Tin Roof* (West Yorkshire Playhouse).

Film and television credits include: *The Fat Slags* (Funny Films), *Modern Toss* (Channel X), *The Hollow* (Hollow Pictures), *A Woman of Substance* (Channel 4), *Doctors, Absolute Power, Swiss Toni, The Queen's Nose, Jonathan Creek, The Fast Show, Ted* and *Ralph* (BBC), *The Famous Five* (Zenith TV), *Hercule Poirot's Christmas* (Carnival Films), *Coronation Street, The Bill, Breathless* and *Mr Selfridge* (ITV).

Radio credits include: *Married, The Patrick and Maureen Maybe Music Experience, Mr Finchley Goes to Paris, The Russia House* and *Weekending*.

CREATIVE TEAM

PADDY CAMPBELL Writer

Paddy is a Northern Irish writer based in Newcastle upon Tyne. In 2007 he completed Live Theatre's Introduction to Playwriting course and has worked extensively with Live Theatre since.

Wet House is Paddy's first full length play. His other work with Live Theatre includes *Day of the Flymo, Dial a Mate, The Potting Pelaw Python, I Just Feel So Special, Home Help, Angel 2106, The Group, Perjury* and *Tis The Season.* He has also had work produced there in co-productions with National Theatre (*The Great Unwashed*) and nabokov (*The Nest*).

Paddy has also worked as a dramaturg on Live Theatre's young writer's projects, First Draft and Write Stuff. His plays for other companies include *Flowerpet* (GIFT Festival), *One Small Case* and *My New Favourite Place* (Curious Monkey), *Breaking Point* (Northumbrian Touring Theatre), *The Conceptualist's Mam* (Ink Festival) and *School Run* (Sage Gateshead).

MAX ROBERTS Director

Max is the Artistic Director and a founding member of Live Theatre. His directing credits include new plays by some of the finest writers from the North East including: CP Taylor, Tom Hadaway, Alan Plater, Phil Woods, Julia Darling, Shelagh Stephenson, Peter Straughan, Lee Hall and Michael Chaplin.

Max was delighted to direct *Wet House* for Live Theatre's 40th anniversary season alongside *Tyne* by Michael Chaplin and a revival of Lee Hall's *Cooking with Elvis,* a play he first directed for Live Theatre 16 years ago. In 2014, Max directed a series of rehearsed readings of screenplays by Lee Hall (and Simon Beaufoy) as well as Live Theatre's new production *Good Timin'.*

GARY MCCANN Designer

Gary trained at Nottingham Trent University.

His design credits for theatre and opera include: *The Pitmen Painters* (Live Theatre/National Theatre Broadway, Volkstheater Vienna and Bill Kenright Ltd West End and national tours), *The Girl in the Yellow Dress* (Live Theatre/ Citizens Theatre/Market Theatre, Johannesburg, Stadttheater Stockholm and Baxter Theatre, Capetown), *The Barber of Seville, La Voix Humaine* and *L'Heure Espagnole* (Nationale Reisopera, Holland), *Die Fledermaus* (Norwegian National Opera), *The Flying Dutchman* (Ekaterinburg State Opera, Russia), *Three Days in May, Dangerous Corner* (Bill Kenwright), *33 Variations* (Volkstheater Vienna), *Guys and Dolls* (Theater Bielefeld, Germany), *Fidelio* (Garsington Opera), *Cosi Fan Tutte* (Schönbrunn Palace, Vienna), *Norma* (National Opera of Moldova), *Imeneo* (London Handel Festival), *Faramondo* (Göttingen Festspiele Germany), *Owen Wingrave* and *La Pietra Del Paragone* (Opera Trionfo, Amsterdam). His work has been exhibited at the V&A museum in London - as part of the Collaborators and Transformation & Revelation exhibitions.

ABOUT LIVE THEATRE

From its base on Newcastle's quayside, Live Theatre produces work as varied and diverse as the audiences it engages with. To do this it:

- Creates and performs new plays of world class quality
- Finds and develops creative talent
- Unlocks the potential of young people through theatre.

Founded in 1973, the Theatre was transformed in 2007 with a capital redevelopment. The result is a beautifully restored and refurbished complex of five Grade II listed buildings with state-of-the-art facilities in a unique historical setting, including a 160-seat cabaret-style theatre, a studio theatre, renovated rehearsal rooms, a series of dedicated writers' rooms as well as a thriving café, bar and pub.

Live Theatre is a national leader in developing new strategies for increasing income and assets for the charity. In 2014 the company announced LiveWorks, a £10 million capital development to purchase and develop quayside-fronted land and buildings adjacent to the Theatre, to create new commercial office space, a public park and a children and young people's writing centre.

LiveWorks will join the award-winning pub The Broad Chare, online course www.beaplaywright.com and The Schoolhouse (an office space for SMEs), as one of Live Theatre's creative enterprises, which increases funds through new income streams.

For more information see **www.live.org.uk**

Through the generosity of our Friends Live Theatre is able to continue to nurture and develop new writing talent, and deliver plays of world class quality. Our Best Friends are:

Noreen Bates
Jim Beirne
Michael & Pat Brown
Paul Callaghan
George Caulkin
Michael & Susan Chaplin
Sue & Simon Clugston
Helen Coyne
Chris Foy
Robson Green
Lee Hall
John Jordan
John Josephs
Annette Marlowe
Elaine Orrick
Ian & Christine Shepherdson
Margaret & John Shipley
Sting
Shelagh Stephenson
Peter Straughan
Alan Tailford
Graeme & Aly Thompson
Paul & Julie Tomlinson
Nick & Melanie Tulip
Alison Walton
Kevin Whately & Madelaine Newton
Lucy Winskell

For more information about the Friends of Live Theatre please contact Lizzy Skingley on **(0191) 269 3498** or **lizzy@live.org.uk**

Live Theatre is grateful for the support of Arts Council England and Newcastle City Council as well as its many other supporters.

STAFF AT LIVE THEATRE

Chief Executive Jim Beirne
Artistic Director Max Roberts
Operations Director Wendy Barnfather
Director of Enterprise & Development Lucy Bird
Director of Education & Engagement Helen Moore
Administrator, Directors Clare Overton
Literary Manager Gez Casey
Creative Producer Graeme Thompson
Administrator, Literary Team Degna Stone
Associate Director, Literary Team Steve Gilroy
Production Manager Drummond Orr
Technical Manager Dave Flynn
Technician Hannah Gregory
Technician Sam Stewart
Technical Apprentice Craig Spence
Associate Director, Education & Participation Paul James
Drama Worker Rachel Glover
Drama Worker Philip Hoffmann
Administrator, Education & Participation Sam Bell
Marketing Manager (Job Share) Claire Cockroft
Marketing Manager (Job Share) Cait Read
Marketing & Press Officer Emma Hall
Marketing & Press Assistant Melanie Rashbrooke
Box Office Administrator Amy Foley
Development Manager Lizzy Skingley
Events & Hires Administrator Chris Foley
Finance Manager Antony Robertson
Finance Officer Catherine Moody
Finance Assistant Helen Tuffnell
House Manager Carole Wears
Deputy House Manager Michael Davies
Duty House Manager Ben Young
Duty House Manager Mark Gerrens
Duty House Manager Lewis Jobson

Front of House & Box Office Staff
Nina Berry, Camille Burridge, Lee Johnson, Roisin Linton,
Caroline Liversidge, Sarah Matthews, Emily Merritt, Hannah Murphy,
Matilda Neill, Tilly Riley, Alisdair Robertson and Molly Wright.

London's most vibrant venue for new theatre, comedy and cabaret.

Soho Theatre is a major creator of new theatre, comedy and cabaret. Across our three different spaces we curate the finest live performance we can discover, develop and nurture. Soho Theatre works with theatre makers and companies in a variety of ways, from full producing of new plays, to co-producing new work, working with associate artists and presenting the best new emerging theatre companies that we can find.

We have numerous writers and theatre makers on attachment and under commission, six young writers and comedy groups and we read and see hundreds of shows a year – all in an effort to bring our audience work that amazes, moves and inspires.

'Soho Theatre was buzzing, and there were queues all over the building as audiences waited to go into one or other of the venue's spaces. [The audience] is so young, exuberant and clearly anticipating a good time.' *Guardian*

We attract over 170,000 audience members a year. We produced, co-produced or staged over forty new plays in the last twelve months.

Our social enterprise business model means that we maximise value from Arts Council and philanthropic funding; we actually contribute more to government in tax and NI than we receive in public funding.

sohotheatre.com

Keep up to date:
sohotheatre.com/mailing-list
facebook.com/sohotheatre
twitter.com/sohotheatre
youtube.com/sohotheatre

Registered Charity No: 267234

Soho Theatre, 21 Dean Street
London W1D 3NE
Admin 020 7287 5060
Box Office 020 7478 0100

Supported using public funding by
ARTS COUNCIL ENGLAND

THANK YOU

We are immensely grateful to our fantastic Soho Theatre Friends and Supporters. Soho Theatre is supported by Arts Council England.

Principal Supporters
Nicholas Allott, Hani Farsi, Jack and Linda Keenan, Amelia and Neil Mendoza, Lady Susie Sainsbury, Carolyn Ward, Jennifer and Roger Wingate

The Soho Circle
Celia Atkin, Giles Fernando, Michael and Jackie Gee, Hedley and Fiona Goldberg, Isobel and Michael Holland, Tim Macready

Corporate Supporters
Bargate Murray, Bates Wells & Braithwaite, Cameron Mackintosh Ltd, Financial Express, Fisher Productions Ltd, Fosters, The Groucho Club, Hall & Partners, John Lewis Oxford Street, Latham & Watkins LLP, Lionsgate UK, The Nadler Hotel, Nexo, Oberon Books Ltd, Overbury Leisure, Publicis, Quo Vadis, Soho Estates, Soundcraft, SSE Audio Group

Trusts & Foundations
The Andor Charitable Trust, The Austin and Hope Pilkington Charitable Trust, Backstage Trust, Bertha Foundation, Boris Karloff Charitable Foundation, Bruce Wake Charitable Trust, The Buzzacott Stuart Defries Memorial Fund, The Charles Rifkind and Jonathan Levy Charitable Settlement, The City of Westminster Charitable Trust, The Coutts Charitable Trust, The David and Elaine Potter Foundation, The D'Oyly Carte Charitable Trust, The Ernest Cook Trust, The Edward Harvist Trust, The 8th Earl of Sandwich Memorial Trust, Equity Charitable Trust, The Eranda Foundation, Esmée Fairbairn Foundation, The Fenton Arts Trust, The Foundation for Sport and the Arts, The Foyle Foundation, Harold Hyam Wingate Foundation, Help A London Child, Hyde Park Place Estate Charity, The Ian Mactaggart Trust, John Ellerman Foundation, John Lewis Oxford Street Community Matters Scheme, John Lyon's Charity, The John Thaw Foundation, JP Getty Jnr Charitable Trust, The Kobler Trust, The Mackintosh Foundation, The Mohamed S. Farsi Foundation, The Rose Foundation, The Royal Victoria Hall Foundation, St Giles-in-the-Fields and William Shelton Educational Charity, The St James's Piccadilly Charity, Teale Charitable Trust, The Theatres Trust, The Thistle Trust, Unity Theatre Charitable Trust, Westminster City Council-West End Ward Budget, The Wolfson Foundation

Soho Theatre Best Friends
Nick Bowers, Johan and Paris Christofferson, Richard Collins, Miranda Curtis, Norma Heyman, Beatrice Hollond, David King, Lady Caroline Mactaggart, Jesper Nielsen and Hannah Soegaard-Christensen, Hannah Pierce, Amy Ricker, Ian Ritchie and Jocelyne van den Bossche, Ann Stanton, Alex Vogel, Sian and Matthew Westerman, Hilary and Stuart Williams

Soho Theatre Dear Friends
David Aukin, Natalie Bakova, Norman Bragg, Neil and Sarah Brener, Cherry and Rob Dickins, Manu Duggal, Jonathan Glanz, Alban Gordon, Jane Henderson, Shappi Khorsandi, Jeremy King, Lynne Kirwin, Michael Kunz, Anita and Brook Land, Jonathan Levy, Nick Mason and Annette Lynton Mason, Ryan Miller, Mark and Carolyn Mishon, Lauren Prakke, Phil and Jane Radcliff, Sue Robertson, Dominic and Ali Wallis, Andrea Wong, Garry Watts, Matt Woodford, Christopher Yu

Soho Theatre Good Friends
Oladipo Agboluaje, Jonathan and Amanda Baines, Indigo Carnie, Alison Carr, Chris Carter, Rosalie Carter, Stephen Cavell, Natasha Clendinnen, Vivienne Clore, Jeremy Conway, Deborah D'Arcy, Sharon Eva Degen, David Dolman, Geoffrey and Janet Eagland, Will Farrell, Denzil and Renata Fernandez, Wendy Fisher, Gail and Michael Flesch, Sue Fletcher, James Flitton, Daniel and Joanna Friel, Kathryn Gardner, Stephen Garrett - Kudos Films, Alex Hardy, Michelle Harrison, Doug Hawkins, Anthony Hawser, Etan Ilfeld, Eloise Jacobs, Ed Kelly, Julie Knight, Clive Laing, David and Linda Lakhdhir, Charlotte MacLeod, Jo MacGregor, Amanda Mason, Neil Mastrarrigo, Gerry McGrail, Andrew and Jane McManus, Mike Miller, Mike Miller, Glyn Morgan, Mr and Mrs Roger Myddelton, Martin Ogden, Alan Pardoe, David Pelham, James Pembroke, Fiona and Gary Phillips, Edward Pivcevic, Alison Rae, Stephanie Ressort, Helen Rowe, Dan Savidge, Barry Serjent, Lesley Symons, Liz Young

We would also like to thank those supporters who wish to stay anonymous as well as all of our Soho Theatre Friends. Soho Theatre has the support of the Channel 4 Playwrights' Scheme sponsored by Channel 4 Television.

Wet House

by Paddy Campbell

FOR AMATEUR PRODUCTION ENQUIRIES

UNITED KINGDOM AND WORLDWIDE, EXCLUDING USA AND CANADA

plays@SamuelFrench-London.co.uk

020 7255 4302/01

Each title is subject to availability from Samuel French, depending
upon country of performance.

For my parents.

CHARACTERS

SETTING

A homeless hostel in North East England. It is a wet hostel where residents can drink alcohol on the premises.

NOTE

A / denotes a suggested point of overlap between that line and the next actor's line.

During scene changes the CCTV monitor can be used to show the monotony of the work and the lives of the hostel residents. For example, the same staff member mops the same corridor, the same resident trying and failing to get his key in his door and falling over. The CCTV will be on during scenes in the office.

Preferably the actors should make any necessary changes to the set during scene changes. Mopping up spillages and clearing away breakages showing the nature of hostel work.

ACT I

Scene One

(The hostel office. There are two doors, each has a window with one way glass so people in the office can see out but people can't see in. There is a desk, three chairs, a filing cabinet and shelves full of files and folders. There is a CCTV monitor on a bracket on the wall and an intercom system, the screen changes between images of empty corridors and a large basic dining room with men drinking. The sound made by a room full of drunken men can be heard in the background. HELEN sits at the desk writing in the log book. There is a mug of coffee and an ashtray at the other end of the desk. MIKE enters and throws himself on the seat, leans forward with his head in his hands and breathes heavily for a few moments. HELEN continues writing. MIKE sits up and looks at the coffee.)

MIKE. Mine?

HELEN. Don't mention it.

(MIKE drinks some coffee.)

MIKE. Where's Jim?

HELEN. Sick.

MIKE. What d'ye mean sick?

HELEN. Rang in sick.

MIKE. Sick! Sick my hole. Bastard!

HELEN. Shitting through the eye of a needle he said.

MIKE. Who's coming in? Not Martin, if it's Martin I'm straight out the door this second.

1

HELEN. It's not Martin.

MIKE. Do you know what he said to me last time? I swear
     I was that close, that close.

HELEN. What?

MIKE. Unbelievable, we're sat in the lounge right, and for
     once, for once things are nice and quiet. And I'm
     just sat reading the paper, enjoying the peace. And
     Martin comes in and says, do ye mind if I watch the
     golf? Not at all Martin, you watch away there, I'm just
     gonna sit here, read the paper and enjoy the peace.
     Then he says, have you been watching the golf? And
     I say, Martin, I can't think of anything in the entire
     universe I could give less of a fuck about than golf, but
     you watch away there.

     And I didn't say it antagonistic, or anything like that.
     But at the same time making it absolutely one hundred
     per cent clear that I have no interest in golf. So we're
     sitting there, and once or twice, out loud, he goes.
     Nice drive, or, lovely putt. Which is pretty seriously
     irritating. But I don't say anything, I let that go. And
     then he goes, wait'll you hear this. Then he says to
     me. If Hernandez goes on to win this he'll be the first
     player in fifty years to win a major championship with
     a beard.

     (Pause.)

     I couldn't believe it. Could not believe what had just
     come out of his mouth. I mean I'm a laid back person.

HELEN. You're a laid back person?

MIKE. Serenity's my middle name.

HELEN. Raul Moat with crabs would be more relaxed than
     you at the best of times.

MIKE. Bollocks! Anyway right, so he says that, and it takes
     everything within me not to put his head through the
     TV there and then.

     What!? I said, and he says it again. If Hernandez wins
     this he'll be the first player in fifty years to win a major
     tournament with a beard.

(Slight pause.)

I said Martin, why? Why in the name of Christ are you telling me that? Just making conversation, he says. Just making conversation! I've just made it explicitly fucking clear to the man that I haven't the remotest interest in golf. That I would like to sit and read the paper in peace. And what does he do? Decides it would be a good idea to try and start a conversation with me about a bearded golfer I've never heard of, and the history of bearded golfers winning fucking golf tournaments. The man's a retard. If I'd killed him there, I'd have got diminished responsibility, no question. In fact surely there's instances when the provocation someone's put under justifies it. Jesus, I could punch something thinking about it.

(Pause.)

HELEN. Do you ever question your decision to pursue a career in the care industry?

MIKE. What's wrong with people, seriously? Who's coming in anyway?

HELEN. It's a surprise.

MIKE. I don't like surprises, just tell us who it is.

HELEN. No it's actually a surprise. A new recruit, his first day in the fun house.

MIKE. You're joking.

HELEN. You'll have a great day.

MIKE. No…no you're…that's not even…

HELEN. Seems like a lovely boy, youse'll get on like a house on fire.

MIKE. Piss off…this is…this/ is a…

HELEN. He hasn't had his induction yet, but I said you'd have no problem doing that with him.

MIKE. For Christ sake Helen look at the state of me, I'm… I'm still half cut from last night.

HELEN. You'll love it, passing on all your skills and knowledge to a young man eager to learn.

MIKE. This isn't funny.

HELEN. Nonsense.

MIKE. Well where is he? He's late. Ring him, tell him not to bother. I'd rather do it on my own. I would, seriously. Twelve hours, I don't deserve this. Ring him, tell him it's a mistake. I'll do it on my own.

HELEN. He's on his way. He's coming on his bike.

MIKE. He's coming on his bike!

HELEN. Yes, he's coming on his bike.

MIKE. Coming on a bike. This just gets better and better.

HELEN. People ride bikes.

MIKE. I know people ride bikes. I've seen them, on their bikes. I know what sort of people ride bikes. He'll either be a panda saving twat, a lycra fitness twat, or some form of raspberry tea drinking tantric twat. Either way, I don't want to work with him for the next twelve hours. I'd rather work with Martin.

HELEN. Just keep him in here, get him to read policies and procedures.

MIKE. Then I'll have to deal with them, out there. I refuse deal with them out there.

HELEN. This is work, you have to deal with them.

MIKE. Bollocks this is work. I have a gentleman's agreement with Jim when it comes to this particular shift.

HELEN. You and Jim, gentlemen?

MIKE. We do a week on, a week off, getting shitfaced before this shift. One does the work, the other sleeps in the kitchen. It's my week to sleep in the kitchen. I can barely fucking stand.

HELEN. Boo hoo.

MIKE. You're a cruel and heartless woman.

(The doorbell rings and the CCTV monitor shows **ANDY** *in the porch way with his bike.)*

Oh look, he's off his stabilisers.

HELEN. *(buzzing him in)* Come in Andy, through the main doors, down the corridor, and it's the office door on the left.

ANDY. *(through the intercom)* Right OK.

MIKE. *(impersonating* **HELEN***)* Come in Andy, through the main doors, love you already.

HELEN. Behave yourself.

*(**ANDY** enters pushing his bike and carrying a bicycle helmet.)*

MIKE. *(brimming with cheer)* Morning. Have a nice cycle?

ANDY. Yeah, good thanks.

MIKE. Oh good. I'm Mike.

*(**MIKE** extends his hand and they shake hands.)*

ANDY. Andy.

HELEN. Hi Andy, I'm Helen.

ANDY. Hello. Sorry I'm a bit late.

MIKE. Not a problem Andy, no problem whatsoever.

HELEN. Would you like a tea or coffee Andy?

ANDY. Have you any camomile tea, or a peppermint?

*(**MIKE** makes a gesture of utter despair behind **ANDY**'s back.)*

HELEN. Sorry pet, just regular.

ANDY. That's ok.

MIKE. I've been saying we must restock our herbal infusion cupboard as a matter of urgency.

HELEN. Well I'll start the handover then and you and you can sort out the herbal tea situation later on Mike.

Andy, why don't you lock your bike up in the Meds room across the corridor.

*(**HELEN** hands him a bunch of keys.)*

It's the yellow key, the door straight opposite.

ANDY. Ok, cheers.

*(**ANDY** exits pushing his bike.)*

MIKE. This is not happening. Twelve hours with the fucking Milky Bar kid.

HELEN. Seems like a lovely boy.

MIKE. I'm going, fuck it, I don't care.

HELEN. It'll fly by.

MIKE. No, I'm off. Tell em swine flu, anything.

(**ANDY** *enters.*)

(*to himself*) Oh Jesus.

HELEN. Take a seat Andy.

ANDY. Thanks.

(**ANDY** *sits at the desk.*)

HELEN. Right, at the start of each shift we do a hand over, where we just go down the list of residents and say what they've done during the shift.

MIKE. It's gripping stuff Andy.

HELEN. Room A, Reggie, same as ever. Got up, drank till he was making tractor noises, went to bed. He's having his morning bottle out there now.

Lee's in police custody, shop lifting yesterday.

MIKE. Again.

HELEN. The Colonel pissed on his mobility scooter.

MIKE. Again.

HELEN. He's gonna end up electrocuting himself.

MIKE. Again.

HELEN. Bungle scared the shit out of me. I went into the bathroom and he's just stood there staring, bollock naked, bolt upright in the empty bath. I asked if he was alright, and he growled at me then said the Egyptians were coming for his eyes.

MIKE. Bungle's great Andy, he's absolutely howling at the moon. He went out the back last month, pulled a bird table out of the ground and charged full pelt at the greenhouse. Cut himself to ribbons. We've still got it on CCTV, I'll show you later. It's a classic.

HELEN. Oh it's hilarious.

MIKE. Come on, it is funny.

HELEN. Dinger was in good form all night, singing show tunes, then did a dying swan act on the lounge floor, where he's still lying in a heap. I think he's achieved the double.

MIKE. Go on Dinger.

ANDY. What's the double?

HELEN. Double incontinent, he's pissed and shat himself.

ANDY. Oh right.

HELEN. Kerry was a complete pain in the arse. Trying to cadge drink and tabs off everyone, and screeching the place down. She's gone out this morning to beg at the Metro. Reckons she gets twice as much now the babies showing.

MIKE. She's not getting back in, I'm serious.

HELEN. Luke just hit pool balls about on his own all night. Room J is a new arrival. Ryan Drake, twenty four, alcoholic, half his liver's knackered already.

MIKE. That's good going.

HELEN. Yeah, pretty impressive. Brian's still missing.

MIKE. Hopefully dead.

HELEN. Mike!

MIKE. What?

HELEN. No fair enough actually.

Danger Mouse was gouging in lounge all evening, as was Soupy.

ANDY. Gouging?

(**MIKE** *sighs gives a* **HELEN** *a look showing his impatience.*)

HELEN. What they call it when they're off it on heroin. Mack is still hanging in there, and just has to make it to Tuesday and you will owe me a fiver Mike.

MIKE. He can't be.

HELEN. He is, the whole corridor reeks of death, but my
fella's refusing to give up the ghost.

Room Q's empty.

Brendan fell asleep in his lasagne. And that completes
the line up, so if you both feel suitably handed over
I am going to flee this hell hole. Bye Andy, enjoy, ta ra.

ANDY. Bye.

MIKE. Bye.

(HELEN *exits. Pause.*)

It's a piece of piss, honestly. Who interviewed you?

ANDY. The manager Ian, and is it Dianne?

MIKE. Area manager, big fatty, looks like a hippo in a frock?

ANDY. That sounds like her.

MIKE. They're clueless the pair of them. Ignore everything
they told you.

ANDY. Right.

MIKE. There's nowt to it, honestly. Hopeless the lot of
them, complete lost causes. Just don't take any shite,
don't let them take the piss.

ANDY. Ok. How long have you been doing it?

MIKE. Too bloody long, bout four years. You done much in
this line?

ANDY. Not really, just finished uni.

MIKE. You'll be right at home here then professor,
intellectual heavy weights the lot of em.

ANDY. I'm not exactly... I mean I wouldn't say...

(*There's a knock at the door.*)

MIKE. Fuck off.

DINGER. (*from off*) You fuck off.

(DINGER *enters.*)

Sorry Michael, any dumps?

(DINGER *looks at* ANDY.)

MIKE. Fill your boots.

(**MIKE** *passes* **DINGER** *the ash tray.*)

DINGER. You movin in son, lend us a tab?

ANDY. No I don't smoke, I'm just starting.

MIKE. Jesus Dinger does he look like one of youse? Does he?

DINGER. What are ye tryin to say?

MIKE. Hasn't shit himself for a start.

(*Slight pause.*)

DINGER. Good point that. Eh, and not with those teeth. They'd blind ye.

(**DINGER** *picks the butts from the ashtray and puts them in a tobacco tin.*)

MIKE. Andy is a man of education, a professor in…what you a professor in?

ANDY. I'm not a professor, I just done a BA in art history.

MIKE. Art history, d'ye hear that?

DINGER. I'm an artist like. Piss artist.

(**DINGER** *offers his hand to* **ANDY**.)

Welcome, I'm Dinger.

(**ANDY** *shakes his hand.*)

ANDY. Andy.

DINGER. Fucking enchanted.

(**MIKE** *laughs.* **ANDY** *wipes his hand on his trousers.*)

MIKE. Right piss off Dinger. I need to tell Andy what's involved in working in this dump.

DINGER. Good luck son, ha. Welcome to Crabtree House.

(**DINGER** *exits and farts as he does so.*)

MIKE. Art history eh.

ANDY. Aye cocked it up.

MIKE. Least you're not a trainee social worker. So what brings you to the care industry? And please don't tell me you want to make a difference.

ANDY. Do you know Sam who worked here?

MIKE. Hippy Sam, good lad Sam.

ANDY. I'm a mate of his, he said it's alright to tide you over.

MIKE. Aye, he's a sound lad Sam, soft as shite like. Where'd he piss off to?

ANDY. He's volunteering in a monkey sanctuary in Bolivia.

MIKE. Same thing as here then. But with sunshine and cheap coke.

Right keys, here's your keys.

(MIKE *hands him a bunch of keys.*)

Lock everything behind you, they'd steal your kidneys if you stood still long enough.

ANDY. Right.

MIKE. That's the main thing. We give em breakfast and dinner, and call the police if there's any kick off. The rest is all bollocks really, support plans, key working, all utter shite. An elaborate exercise in box ticking.

ANDY. Right.

(*Long pause.* MIKE *stretches.*)

And umm…is there anything that I should do? Introduce myself, so that…

MIKE. (*Incredulous*) Introduce yourself! Jesus. Introduce yourself. You could if you want. I generally try to have as little to do with em as possible.

ANDY. You don't think I should?

MIKE. No no, by all means. That's good, not phased, you shouldn't be phased.

ANDY. I'm not phased, just thought it might be, you know, good to introduce myself.

MIKE. I can't remember the last time I had any inclination to willingly talk to a ressie.

ANDY. Ressie?

MIKE. Resident, knacker, degenerate, human puss. And they all are in some form or another. Not always at first, but given time the Crabtree effect takes hold. Enough time spent in here and anyone, anyone without fail, will descend into something that could never possibly be described as a normal person.

(The doorbell rings. We see **KERRY**, *drunk and pregnant, with a bottle of cider swaying at the front door on the CCTV monitor.)*

Ah the lovely Kerry. Watch this.

(MIKE *presses a button on the intercom and talks into it.)*

The door's open Kerry, come on in. *(to* **ANDY***)* It's not like.

(We see **KERRY** *try the door which does not open.)*

KERRY. *(screeching through intercom)* OPEN THE FUCKING DOOR NOW YOU BASTARD!

MIKE. It's open Kerry.

(We see **KERRY** *violently shake the door then kick it. She throws her bottle at the camera.)*

KERRY. *(screaming)* I'LL FUCKING KILL YOU!

(MIKE *lets go of the intercom button so* **KERRY** *can no longer be heard. She continues to scream into the camera and kick the door.)*

MIKE. *(laughing)* Oh dear.

(MIKE *picks up the telephone, presses a button then speaks.)*

Yes, hello, I'm phoning from Crabtree House. One of our residents is causing a disturbance in our front porch. Her name's Kerry Rice, aye that's the one. Well, she's just returned heavily under influence of alcohol and has tried to smash one of our security cameras. She's now making threats to kill myself, and is trying to kick the front door down.

(Pause.)

MIKE. Aye it's Mike.

Not bad, you know.

(Pause.)

Thank you. Bye.

*(**MIKE** hangs up the phone.)*

One down. Officers en route. Right, I'm going for a dump, by all means get out there and introduce yourself.

*(**MIKE** exits. **ANDY** looks at the screen which shows **KERRY** who has tired herself out and is slumped against the door.)*

Scene Two

(Corridor. **ANDY** *brushes the floor and* **HELEN** *follows behind him with a mop.)*

ANDY. It's not how I thought it'd be. Interesting though. I didn't really know what to do with myself. Mainly just read their files.

HELEN. That's a barrel of laughs.

ANDY. You really don't think, do you? That that stuff actually... I mean, Reggie's file, Christ, it's no wonder he's...

HELEN. Yeah, it's pretty grim. You'll still want to throttle them all the same.

ANDY. I thought Mike was actually going to. There was a poo on the bathroom floor, and...who's the one with the dints in his head?

HELEN. Ryan.

ANDY. Yeah Ryan. I honestly thought he was going to rub his nose in it. I don't know how he knew it was Ryan, he seemed certain it was. But yeah, Ryan was quite, you know, he looked pretty scared. I don't know if it was Ryan, but he cleaned it up anyway, cos otherwise... I didn't think that...because when you do the interview and the questionnaire, you don't think that's the sort of thing that you'll be doing.

HELEN. No, rubbing people's noses in, poo, isn't generally the sort of thing you'll be doing.

ANDY. I mean, it was quite funny really.

HELEN. I wouldn't, necessarily follow Mike's example.

ANDY. Oh no, I wouldn't. I couldn't do that.

HELEN. Things like that, it's probably not a great thing to be doing.

ANDY. Yeah, no of course. I didn't mean like funny ha ha, but, you know, a bit funny. Do you know what I mean?

HELEN. I'd just be careful, with Mike.

ANDY. Yeah, sure. How do you mean, careful?

HELEN. Just, you know, don't get drawn into anything that could get you in bother.

ANDY. Right, ok.

(Short pause.)

That was just one thing. In general he seemed like a good bloke.

HELEN. Oh he is. I'm just saying to be a bit cautious. Wouldn't want Mike's methods getting you in bother while you're still on probation.

ANDY. No. I mean, I did think that if Ian came in.

HELEN. Ian? On a Sunday?

ANDY. That this probably doesn't look too great.

HELEN. Not a hope in hell Ian would pop in on a Sunday.

ANDY. No?

HELEN. As far as Ian's concerned, if the paper work's up to date then everything's fine. Provided there's a bit of paper filled in saying Reggie's had a key working session, then Reggie could be swinging from rafters for all Ian cares.

ANDY. And, the stuff in the files. Like what happened to Reggie. Do they see anyone, get any kind of help?

HELEN. We are the help. To be honest, Reggie's beyond help. Can't blame him really for wanting to be permanently plastered.

ANDY. Suppose.

HELEN. Some of them do make small improvements, it's hard to see that when you're here day in day out.

ANDY. Ultimately though, do you think it does any good?

HELEN. I don't know, keeps them off the streets, well where else could you put them? Would you fancy Regie living next door?

ANDY. And is that it? Is that all it's for?

HELEN. Well it's something. No one's come up with anything better. Well, nothing affordable, and God knows how long this place'll last.

ANDY. It's kind of like that Dignitas place in Switzerland, but done really slowly and with no pretence of dignity.

HELEN. I wouldn't say that in your supervision.

ANDY. Can't imagine getting to that stage.

HELEN. Probably a lot easier than you think.

ANDY. Still though, to end up like that, where you just don't care.

HELEN. You'll be surprised how quickly you get used to it.

(Several boxes of Marks and **SPENCER** *sandwiches are thrown on stage.)*

KERRY. *(from off)* Jesus what the fucking hell is this?

*(***KERRY*** enters and spits out a mouthful of sandwich.)*

KERRY. What the fuck is this shite?

*(***HELEN*** picks up a box of sandwiches and looks at it.)*

HELEN. They appear to be brie apple and grape in sun dried tomato infused bread.

KERRY. What sort of sick fuck goes putting fruit in sandwiches? Dirty bastards.

HELEN. Just cos you don't like them, is there any need to throw them about the place?

KERRY. They're fucking rotten. Like chewin on a Glade plug in.

HELEN. But still, they are generously donated, and someone else might have had them.

KERRY. They can kindly donate them up their arse. Will you do us some of your cheese on toast?

HELEN. Strictly speaking the kitchen is shut.

KERRY. Please.

HELEN. Well considering your condition I think we can stretch to some cheese on toast.

KERRY. You're a star.

HELEN. Coming up.

ANDY. I can do it if you like.

KERRY. *(to* ANDY*)* Hello gorgeous.

HELEN. No, you're alright.

KERRY. Loads of red sauce.

(HELEN *exits.* ANDY *bends over and starts picking up the boxes of sandwiches.)*

Look at the arse on that.

(KERRY *walks up to him and squeezes his arse.* ANDY *jumps up holding a handful of sandwiches.)*

You new love?

ANDY. *(flustered)* I umm, yes, thanks. We met last Sunday actually.

KERRY. Don't remember that like. Bout time they got a bit of talent in ere. What time you on till?

ANDY. Umm eight.

KERRY. Got ye all night do I? Lucky me.

(ANDY *grins awkwardly and backs away. He goes to pick up the sandwiches he dropped then thinks better of it. Pause.)*

ANDY. When's it due?

KERRY. What?

ANDY. The uhh… *(gestures to her stomach with his hand)* baby.

KERRY. Ye cheeky fucker, I'm not pregnant.

ANDY. *(mortified)* I am so so sorry, I thought Helen said, I was sure she… I'm really sorry.

KERRY. You wanna be fuckin sorry.

ANDY. I am honestly, I'm really sorry.

(KERRY *starts advancing towards* ANDY.*)*

KERRY. Fuckin arsehole.

Why don't you er…give us a kiss to make up for it?

ANDY. I… I…well…

KERRY. Go on, hurting a girl's feelings like that.

ANDY. Sorry, I…umm…

(KERRY makes a grab for ANDY's crotch. ANDY jumps back, panicking.)

KERRY. Don't be shy.

ANDY. Please stop.

KERRY. Are ye a poof or something?

ANDY. No, but…

KERRY. Well come on then.

(KERRY makes another grab for ANDY's crotch getting a good handful this time. She starts to undo his belt. ANDY struggles to fend her off but his hands full of sandwiches.)

ANDY. Wooah, wooooahh!

(KERRY cackles.)

KERRY. Come on mister big stuff.

ANDY. I can't, this is my job…and I'm, I'm spoken for.

(Pause. KERRY stops and steps away from him.)

KERRY. You're, spoken for?

ANDY. Yes.

KERRY. *(laughs uproariously)* Spoken for! Where the fuck did they get you? Fuckin spoken for. Are ye Prince William? Got ye good un there. Your face ye daft bastard. Thought ye were gonna start bublin.

(HELEN enters.)

HELEN. On its way Kerry, if you wanna go round to the hatch.

KERRY. Did ye na this one's, spoken for Helen?

HELEN. You leave him alone missus. Go on round and get your toast.

KERRY. *(as she exits)* Spoken for, fucking class. *(laughs)*

(ANDY adjusts his belt.)

ANDY. She is terrifying.

HELEN. She's lovely, and you've gone beetroot. Just be careful around her.

ANDY. I tried to. And she is…?

HELEN. What?

ANDY. Pregnant.

HELEN. Course she is dafty.

ANDY. Thank God, just she said…

HELEN. Winding you up.

ANDY. Course, yeah.

HELEN. Oh dear.

ANDY. Right. Is she gonna stay here, when she has it?

HELEN. Social worker's trying to get a place in a mother and baby unit.

ANDY. What about the dad?

HELEN. Could be any one of the regulars at The Ben Lomond, and have you seen the burger van outside the industrial estate on the way in?

ANDY. Yeah.

HELEN. Him and his son are another possibility.

ANDY. Jesus.

KERRY. *(screaming from off)* I CAN SMELL IT BURNING YE DAFT COW!

HELEN. Bollocks!

(HELEN *exits quickly.*)

Scene Three

(The kitchen. **HELEN** *is peeling potatoes.* **MIKE** *is drinking from a mug.)*

HELEN. You appear to have made an impression.

MIKE. Yeah?

HELEN. Regale him with tales from the field of conflict?

MIKE. I didn't regale him with tales of any of my conquests.

HELEN. Conflict, I said conflict.

MIKE. That neither.

HELEN. No, I'd say you gained yourself quite a fan.

MIKE. Can't think how. Did my best to put him off. He's not gonna last five minutes.

HELEN. Don't you think?

MIKE. Like a cross between Harry Potter and Clark Kent. He'll get eaten alive.

HELEN. He won't.

MIKE. Wait'll you see.

HELEN. All this eating alive business.

MIKE. Well he will.

HELEN. You've been here as long as me. No one gets eaten alive.

MIKE. Ray.

HELEN. That was nothing to do with here. He was a raving homosexual who got hidings off his wife and cried watching Cash In The Attic.

MIKE. *(mimicking Ray)* My Nanna had that butter dish. She had that…that exact same butter dish.

*(**MIKE** erupts into a fit of over the top sobbing. They both laugh.)*

19

HELEN. He'd've had nervous breakdown working in a mitten shop, let alone here.

MIKE. Still, don't think this kid's cut out for it.

HELEN. One minute you're banging on about how pathetic they all are…

MIKE. They are.

HELEN. Then the next minute they're some sort of ominous force capable of devouring anyone who hasn't served in Kosovo, fought the IRA. You've got to have an enemy, don't you?

MIKE. Bollocks.

HELEN. You do.

MIKE. Ah, is that it?

HELEN. What?

MIKE. I see.

HELEN. What?

MIKE. Entirely predictable.

HELEN. Oh piss off.

MIKE. You're saying this isn't about that?

HELEN. No, this is nothing to do with that.

MIKE. Course it's not.

HELEN. I was just saying…

MIKE. All of a sudden you decide, I know. Let's get Mike on the couch for a spot of amateur psychology.

HELEN. Just saying it doesn't make any sense what you say. It's got nothing to do with that.

MIKE. Coincidence then, the probing questions into my psyche?

HELEN. Hardly probing questions. I was just pointing out that it always seems like you're under siege. You should try to relax a bit.

MIKE. I'm whale song on legs.

HELEN. And I wish you'd stop bringing up that, that…

MIKE. That what?

HELEN. That stupid fucking incident.

MIKE. Stupid, fucking, incident. That's one way to put it.

HELEN. A massive mistake is another, one that won't be repeated.

MIKE. I thought it was magical, the earth moved. Please tell me you found it magical.

HELEN. Look don't, right, just don't.

MIKE. Don't what?

HELEN. I'm sorry I opened my mouth.

MIKE. I'm not sorry you opened your mouth.

HELEN. Prick!

MIKE. In fact any time you feel like opening your mouth/ again…

HELEN. Not gonna happen.

Tosser!

Scene Four

(The office. **MIKE** *and* **ANDY**. **MIKE** *takes a bottle of whiskey from the bottom drawer of the filing cabinet.)*

MIKE. Livener?

ANDY. What? Whiskey. No.

MIKE. Go on there.

*(**MIKE** pours some into his mug.)*

ANDY. Honestly I'm alright.

MIKE. Nonsense. You need it in this place, take my word for it.

ANDY. Maybe when I've found my feet a bit. Know what I'm doing a bit better.

MIKE. There's nowt to it. Get a drop down ye.

ANDY. I know but still.

MIKE. Take the edge off.

ANDY. Honestly.

MIKE. Go on.

ANDY. Really, I'm alright.

MIKE. Suit yourself.

ANDY. Just a drop.

*(**MIKE** pours a large measure into **ANDY**'s coffee.)*

That's enough.

MIKE. Thought you were meant to be a student.

(There's a knock at the door, **ANDY** *stands to open it.)*

Leave it.

ANDY. Leave it?

MIKE. Aye, leave it. I told him we'd things to sort out, he can wait.

ANDY. Ok.

(Pause. There's another knock at the door, more urgent.)

MIKE. We're not fucking here to jump every fucking time they click their fingers, specially this fucking tosser. Why should we?

(More knocking.)

Bastard.

(MIKE *puts the whiskey in the filing cabinet.*)

Watch and learn.

(MIKE *opens the door.* SPENCER *enters, his shirt front is soaking. He carries a clear plastic bag containing clothes and possessions.*)

SPENCER. *(irate)* Some fuckin…funny fucker…just fuckin… covered us in piss.

MIKE. Whoa Spencer whoa, language please. You're turning the air blue there.

ANDY. What's happened Spencer?

SPENCER. I… I…some bastard….

MIKE. Spencer.

SPENCER. Look at the fucking state of this.

MIKE. Spencer if you don't moderate your language I will have to ask you to leave the office.

SPENCER. Bloody soaked.

MIKE. Has there been some form of mishap?

SPENCER. One of them…chucked it all down us.

ANDY. Did you see who?

MIKE. No surely not.

SPENCER. Came up behind us, bloody drenched in piss.

MIKE. They're a good bunch of lads, sound as a pound.

SPENCER. I'm tellin ye…some…some…

MIKE. Must've been an accident.

SPENCER. Don't be daft.

(MIKE steps up close to SPENCER.)

MIKE. I'd advise you not to call me daft Spencer.

SPENCER. Sorry, I didn't mean… I just want to keep me head down.

MIKE. I bet you do.

ANDY. Should we umm, get this done?

MIKE. Do you believe you've been the victim of bullying Spencer? Cus we have a strict bullying policy. I've been on a course.

(Pause.)

Well Spencer?

(Slight pause.)

You could phone the police, there's a pay phone out there, nine nine nine's free. I'm sure they'll treat it with the utmost urgency.

(Slight pause.)

No. Well we can't stand here all day. On with the induction then. Sit.

*(**SPENCER** sits. **MIKE** drops a key in front of **SPENCER**.)*

Here's your key, Room Q top of the stairs turn right, end of the corridor. You'll find a bathroom further down the corridor. Hand your key into staff each time you go out, if you lose it you pay for it. Front door's locked at all times you need to get one of us to open it for you. Breakfast seven thirty to nine dinner four to six thirty. No alcohol in the dining room during meal times. Residents are expected to be in their rooms by twelve thirty when all communal areas are shut down. Oops forgot any dietary requirements, allergies? No? Good. How do you take your steak? Rare, medium? Only joking. Right next, medication. You on any medication?

SPENCER. Aye I've, I've got these.

*(**SPENCER** starts rummaging through his bag.)*

MIKE. If you want we can look after medication for you in here or you can administer yourself.

(**SPENCER** *sets two boxes of tablets on the desk.* **MIKE** *picks them up and reads.*)

Thiamine and, ooh Zopiclone. Trouble sleeping? Wonder why? You're alright sorting your own meds out aren't ye Spencer? Good man, less paper work for us.

Key worker. Each service user will be allocated a key worker. Right I'm your key worker Spencer, how do you do? I'm Mike. Any problems, you come to me.

Rules, I'll just do the main ones. Violence, abusive or threatening behaviour directed towards staff or other residents may result in immediate eviction.

Do you take drugs?

SPENCER. No…

MIKE. Good.

Visitors. No visitors apart from professionals, social worker, probation and the like. Any questions? No, good man. Consider yourself inducted.

(**MIKE** *pushes the form and pen to* **SPENCER**.)

Sign it.

(**SPENCER** *signs.*)

Right we're done.

(*Slight pause.*)

Well fuck off then.

(**MIKE** *gets up and holds the door open for* **SPENCER** *to leave.* **SPENCER** *picks up his bag from the ground and goes to the door.*)

Any problems, don't hesitate, our door is always open.

(**MIKE** *closes the door firmly on* **SPENCER** *then gets the whiskey out of the filing cabinet.*)

MIKE. Every paedophile I have encountered in this place has looked exactly, exactly like your classic paedophile. Every one without fail, may as well where a fucking sash.

ANDY. He's not likely to…getting soaked in piss and all.

MIKE. Likely to what?

ANDY. Complain.

MIKE. *(laughs)* Complain. Not a chance. Who to? His key worker.

ANDY. Do you think he knew that you, not that it was you but…

MIKE. Me what?

ANDY. Well, kind of set him up, with the piss.

MIKE. I didn't set him up. I cannot be held responsible for the actions of these animals.

ANDY. Suppose. Did you read his file?

MIKE. Skimmed it, know all I need to know.

ANDY. The stuff when he was a kid.

MIKE. Didn't bother with that bit. No point.

ANDY. His Mam'd be in the bar, and for a few quid she'd give you the keys to her house and you could take your pick between him and his sister.

MIKE. Must've been before they got a fruit machine put in.

ANDY. Jesus.

MIKE. Alright, fair enough, they've all got sob stories and it's fucked them up. But that doesn't get away from the fact that what's been created is an absolute horrible fucking arse hole and always will be.

ANDY. I know but…

MIKE. What were you expecting? Tuck em in, bed time stories.

ANDY. No but… I mean all the stuff about key working and care plans. Supporting them with training and all that.

MIKE. Waste of time, have you seen them? You see the thing with these is, social services have failed, probation failed, mental health services failed, drug and alcohol services failed. All these professionals with degrees, proper ones, not art history, on three times as much as us. So it's not like they can expect us to step in like knights in shining armour. Never fear Spencer, Mike's here, we'll have your life turned round in no time. No one'll admit it, but they're all fucked. We're just going through the motions. Key working all that, complete bollocks. They get dumped here, we get the housing benefit, it's all about money.

ANDY. Isn't that a bit cynical.

MIKE. Cynical, I'll give you cynical, wait'll you hear this. There was this auld bastard in room S, Rob... Rob Tanners. I checked his room near the end of my shift on a Friday and he's dead on his bed. Grey, eyes open, big fucking string of slabber hangin from his mouth to the floor. Now you find a stiff one, you've gotta ring an ambulance, give a statement, it can drag on for ages. It's Friday night, half an hour till I'm finished. So I go down, write in the log book. Staff checked Rob, snoring soundly. And off I go, happy days. Now, it turned out a few other people couldn't be arsed either and he ends up lying there dead a couple of days, till the room next door made complaints.

(MIKE *pours more whiskey into his mug and then* ANDY's.)

ANDY. Honestly I'm/ alright.

MIKE. Shut up man.

So eventually he gets carted out, and they work out he still owes three days rent, even though he was dead for two them. And Ian, the boss knew this. He still said to me...here's your caring, service user based organisation. He said, when I was clearing his room out, if I came across any money it was to be taken to pay his outstanding rent. Now the shit this bloke's wife and kids went through at the hands of this piss head bastard. And I'm being asked to pocket the only money they're likely to have had out of him for years to pay off his rent while he was fucking dead.

(Pause.)

I've served in Bosnia, three tours in Northern Ireland, and in that time I don't think I was ever asked to do something quite so callous. And that was the Parras... this is the fucking care industry.

(Pause.)

ANDY. And did you...was there any money?

MIKE. Christ, what d'ye take me for?

(Pause.)

I put twenty quid in his wallet before his daughter came for his stuff.

Scene Five

(KERRY's bedroom. KERRY is packing her belongings into black bags. A child's Batman costume is folded on the bed. There is a knock at the door and HELEN enters. She carries a new dressing gown which is folded up.)

HELEN. Thought you might need a hand.

KERRY. Just about done. I haven't got much.

HELEN. Got you this.

KERRY. Thanks.

HELEN. Dressing gown, here.

(HELEN hands the dressing gown to KERRY.)

KERRY. It's soft, thanks.

HELEN. S'alright, nice to have something comfortable.

KERRY. Yeah.

(KERRY puts the dressing gown in a bag.)

HELEN. Thought of any names?

KERRY. Charlotte for a girl. Don't know if it's a lad, don't like lads.

HELEN. Charlotte's nice.

KERRY. Probably no point.

HELEN. You don't know.

KERRY. No chance.

HELEN. Could be the making of you, that place.

KERRY. I'm worse than last time.

HELEN. Just try your best eh.

KERRY. I will. I have been. Not used once, stuck with me script.

HELEN. There you go, you see, if you put your mind to it.

KERRY. Could become a nun for all they care.

HELEN. And you'll have people helping you there. Not like here...you won't be surrounded by it all the time.

KERRY. Suppose.

HELEN. You'll be fine.

KERRY. I don't know.

HELEN. And I'll tell them how hard you've been trying.

KERRY. Will you?

HELEN. Course.

KERRY. You won't mention last month.

HELEN. Well, you got arrested so they'll have heard about that.

KERRY. Fuck sake.

HELEN. That was one slip, apart from that though...

KERRY. They'll have made their minds up already.

HELEN. You've been doing really well.

KERRY. Still though, look at us. D'ye honestly think?

HELEN. You've gotta give it a go.

KERRY. I reckon it's social worker's already got somewhere for it. Shouldn't call it, it, should I?

HELEN. They should at least give you a chance.

KERRY. Would you? Honestly.

HELEN. With the right help, and you were willing to really try, then yeah, I would.

KERRY. I am, but after last time.

HELEN. People can change.

KERRY. Can they?

HELEN. You just need a bit of help. Someone looking out for you.

KERRY. Maybe.

HELEN. And when you're away from the numpties in here.

KERRY. Aye.

(Slight pause.)

Na it's fuckin stupid, hopeless. There's times when, when I think, yeah, I could give this a go. But it's shite,

I know it is, I can't do this, it's a joke, pointless. Stupid
to even think it...

HELEN. So why...? No sorry.

KERRY. Why what?

HELEN. No, nothing.

KERRY. No, go on, why what?

HELEN. Why have you kept it, if...if you knew that...?

KERRY. Fuck knows.

(Pause.)

HELEN. Sorry, it's not my place.

KERRY. It's fair enough. I mean what am I playing at?

HELEN. No, I'm sorry, I shouldn't have...you'll be alright
Kerry.

KERRY. Hope so.

(Pause.)

What about you?

HELEN. What?

KERRY. How many you got?

HELEN. Me, no...none.

KERRY. No? You'd be great. D'ye want this one?

*(KERRY laughs. HELEN tries to join in but is
unconvincing.)*

HELEN. Never really been the right moment.

KERRY. This moment's been planned meticulously. Fucking
great catchment area this.

*(HELEN laughs. Pause. HELEN takes a photograph
of KERRY which is stuck to the wall by her bed with
blu-tack.)*

HELEN. Is that you? Your hair's beautiful.

KERRY. Yeah.

HELEN. How old were you then?

KERRY. Fifteen sixteen, the home took us to Flamingo
Land.

HELEN. You look stunning.

(*Slight Pause.*)

KERRY. D'ye na what? I wish I'd been born a fucking minger. Wish I was boz eyed with a tash, rabbit teeth, so no fucker'd want owt to do with us. Big spotty nose and massive ears. I do.

HELEN. No you don't.

KERRY. Make life a lot simpler.

HELEN. No.

KERRY. Too minging to look at... So no one'd want to...

(*Pause.*)

At least with this, with this in here. There's a chance, chance that something decent can...something that's not just, this. This fuckin mess.

HELEN. You're decent.

KERRY. Am I fuck decent.

HELEN. Course you are.

KERRY. They're right, course they're right. It should be taken off me. Put somewhere good, with good people with a garden, holidays, people who're not fuckin... people who can actually care for something...people who are a million miles away from me and this shit.

(HELEN *puts her arm round* KERRY.)

Get off us, I don't do cuddles.

HELEN. Course you do.

KERRY. I mean it.

(KERRY *gets up. Pause. She gestures to the Batman costume.*)

Look at that.

HELEN. What the hell?

KERRY. Leaving present from Dinger. The bairn'll look bonnie in that he said.

(HELEN *picks up the costume which unrolls to its full length.*)

HELEN. It's age seven to eight.

KERRY. Aye.

HELEN. Who buys…?

KERRY. Doubt he bought it. I think he thinks that's what bairns wear, like for general wearing. He never mentioned dressing up or owt, just says, here, got ye this for the bairn, he'll look bonnie in that.

Can ye imagine, social worker comes round and it's dressed up in an eight year old's Batman costume.

(KERRY *puts it in the bag. It is the last item.*)

HELEN. Only Dinger.

That the lot?

KERRY. Think so. I'm going to bed.

HELEN. I'll say farewell then. It will be alright you know.

(HELEN *hugs* KERRY. KERRY *responds for a moment. They separate.* KERRY *gets into bed.*)

I'll come and see you.

KERRY. Will you?

HELEN. Course. Night pet.

(HELEN *goes to exit and turns the light off.*)

KERRY. *(slight panic)* Light.

HELEN. Sorry.

(HELEN *turns the light back on and exits.*)

Scene Six

(**SPENCER***'s bedroom.* **SPENCER** *sits on the bed drinking a bottle of White Storm cider. There is a plastic bag with cans of strong beer on the bed.* **DINGER** *and* **ANDY** *stand by the bed.*)

DINGER. You've not been out of here in three days. It's like getting pissed with Anne Frank. Here.

(**SPENCER** *drinks.*)

Don't drink it all.

SPENCER. It's mine.

(**DINGER** *takes the bottle from him.*)

DINGER. Leave some for the young un.

ANDY. Wouldn't touch that in a million years. The smell of it.

DINGER. A fine beverage, served me well down the years.

ANDY. You can't actually enjoy it. **DINGER.** White Storm's the nectar of the gods. It's what keeps us looking so young and healthy.

(**DINGER** *drains the bottle and belches.*)

Victory!

(**SPENCER** *opens a can and drinks.*)

ANDY. There's fish, chips, mushy peas down there Spencer, with a rice crispy square for pudding.

(**DINGER** *takes a can, opens it and drinks.*)

DINGER. Like the fucking ambassador's reception down there.

SPENCER. Might get some later.

ANDY. Get it while it's fresh. I made it with my own fair hands you know. I'll be very upset if you don't have some.

SPENCER. I'm fine. Just wanna keep me head down.

DINGER. Should've kept your head down when he chucked that piss at ye. Little tip like.

ANDY. He's not even in.

SPENCER. I'm alright in here for the minute.

DINGER. Could take a walk down to Bede's world. You'd love it down there Andy.

ANDY. Why would I love it?

DINGER. You're a scholar aren't ye? Embrace our region's heritage. That and I can show you my future wife.

ANDY. Future wife?

DINGER. Queen of gift shop.

*(**DINGER** groans lustfully.)*

What do you say Spencer?

SPENCER. Another time maybe.

ANDY. Go on Spencer. Do you good to get out for a bit.

*(**DINGER** sees something out the window.)*

DINGER. Look at that twat. Away down the offy on his mobility scooter.

ANDY. The colonel.

DINGER. Ye fucking fake cripple bastard. There's nowt the matter with his legs, I'm telling ye. And he gets a mobility scooter. I'd let the bastard's tyres down.

ANDY. He's got M.S.

DINGER. Bollocks he does, he's just a piss head like the rest of us.

ANDY. It's a condition.

DINGER. What? Wobbling about walking funny. Alreet then.

*(**DINGER** does a drunken stagger.)*

Well I want a mobility scooter and all then, we should all get one.

ANDY. You don't have M.S.

DINGER. He was dancing about to Petunia Clark at four o'clock this morning. I should know, the bastard's in the room next to us.

What d'ye say Spencer? Me and you get mobility scooters. It'll be like fucking Easy Rider. And we could ambush that bastard on his way back from the shop. He get's five bottles on the front of that thing. We could be down Jarrow high street and across the border to Mexico by the morning.

You in Andy?

ANDY. I'm in.

DINGER. What d'ye say Spencer?

(Slight Pause.)

SPENCER. Lads I, I appreciate it, but I'm not feeling too clever here. Might have a kip. Would yous mind... I'll be down later on.

(Slight Pause.)

DINGER. Ye try your fucking best.

(DINGER goes to exit. As he passes SPENCER he stops and starts to sing Downtown by Petula Clark at SPENCER using his can as a microphone. SPENCER can't help laughing and eventually joins in the chorus as does ANDY. As the song progresses DINGER has less knowledge of the words but makes them up and belts out the chorus. He ends up singing flat on his back on the floor.)

SPENCER. *(during the singing, although enjoying it)* Ah piss off ye daft bastards. For Christ's sake.

(When the singing has finished SPENCER throws himself back on the bed.)

DINGER. Fucking mobility scooter my arse.

Scene Seven

(The office. **ANDY** *is alone in the office franticly pulling open the drawers of the filing cabinet and searching through each one.)*

ANDY. Shite, shite, shite.

*(**MIKE** enters.)*

MIKE. What are you doing?

ANDY. Bollocks.

MIKE. What have you done?

ANDY. This isn't…this is not…

MIKE. Don't tell me.

ANDY. I was sure I…

MIKE. Don't even think about/ telling me…

ANDY. I locked it, I'm sure I locked it.

MIKE. You tit.

ANDY. I definitely…

MIKE. You massive tit.

ANDY. I was five minutes.

MIKE. What's gone?

ANDY. Just the petty cash box, I think.

MIKE. Brilliant. Where did you go?

ANDY. The kitchen, I… I just had some Co Co Pops/ and…

MIKE. And was the office open when you came back?

ANDY. I went to…and then…umm yeah it was.

MIKE. Good work.

*(**ANDY** continues to look through the drawers.)*

ANDY. I'm sure that's all that's gone.

MIKE. Well as long as it's just all the money that's gone, we'll be alright.

ANDY. I'm sure I...

MIKE. I just topped it up this morning.

ANDY. I'm really sorry.

MIKE. Don't apologise.

ANDY. Sorry.

MIKE. It's not me gonna be picking up his P45 in the morning.

ANDY. Shit, do you think they'd...

MIKE. Office door left open, money stolen. You're shafted.

ANDY. Bollocks, what am I meant to do?

MIKE. Dunno.

ANDY. I can't lose this job.

MIKE. Who was out there at the time?

ANDY. I really can't lose/ this...

MIKE. Who was out there?

ANDY. Right umm, Dinger was sat in his usual seat, Brendan was...but he's been passed out on the table, and umm Bungle, and that was it. Brian as well. But he's still there, he hasn't moved.

MIKE. That was it?

ANDY. Yeah.

MIKE. Sure?

ANDY. Yeah pretty sure.

MIKE. Pretty sure?

ANDY. No, I'm sure.

MIKE. Right.

ANDY. Right what?

MIKE. In a minute, you, being new and inexperienced, will pull out this plug to charge your phone, turning off the CCTV. I shall then make some polite enquiries about the whereabouts of the petty cash. You do not, repeat, do not plug the CCTV back in until I am back in here. Got that?

ANDY. Right yeah. Why do the cameras need to go off?

MIKE. There's a chance, a small chance, that slightly more than a friendly chat may be needed. You do not breathe a word to anyone. And if I get it back you owe me big time.

ANDY. Right.

MIKE. Ok.

(**MIKE** *exits.* **ANDY** *waits a while then pulls the plug on the CCTV.*)

Scene Eight

(Corridor. **MIKE** *bangs at* **DINGER**'s *door.)*

MIKE. Dinger!

*(***MIKE*** bangs the door.)*

Mr Bell, a moment of your time please.

*(***MIKE*** bangs the door.)*

Last chance Dinger, ready or not.

*(***DINGER*** opens the door.)*

DINGER. What man?! I was having a kip.

MIKE. Easy way or hard way? Up to you?

*(***SPENCER*** enters, he is drunk.)*

DINGER. What?

MIKE. I haven't time to piss about. Entirely up to you how
we do this.

*(***DINGER*** stands and thinks.)*

Hello Spencer.

Five, four, three, /two…

DINGER. Alreet man, alreet…

*(***DINGER*** goes into his room and returns with the petty
cash box which he hands to* **MIKE**.*)*

Just messin with yis, just messin.

*(***DINGER*** laughs.)*

Wouldn't've kept it.

*(***MIKE*** laughs and then* **SPENCER**.*)*

MIKE. Course you wouldn't Dinger. Course not.

DINGER. Bet the young un's shittin a brick is he?

MIKE. He's in that office now, turning the place upside down. His little Joe Ninety glasses all steamed up.

(DINGER and SPENCER laugh.)

What's that **SPENCER**?

SPENCER. *(still laughing)* What?

MIKE. Thought you said something.

SPENCER. No.

MIKE. I'm sure you did.

SPENCER. No I...just laughed.

MIKE. Just laughed.

(MIKE laughs.)

Just laughed. Aye, we have a laugh in here all right. Don't we Dinger?

DINGER. Aye.

MIKE. It's a laugh a fucking minute in here Spencer.

(MIKE laughs.)

DINGER. I didn't mean no harm by it. Just...ye na.

MIKE. No harm done. And it's entertained Spencer. Good to put a smile on Spencer's face. Guy like Spencer.

Give us another laugh there Spencer.

(Slight Pause.)

Go on. We're all having a good laugh aren't we?

DINGER. All sorted now Mike. No harm done.

MIKE. No it's just, just nice to see Spencer smiling. Made my day, putting a smile on Spencer's face. Come on Spencer.

SPENCER. I, uh...

MIKE. Guy like Spencer. Great to see him smiling. Specially after his spell inside, lovely to see him with a smile on his face. Cus that's what I'm here for eh Dinger, to cheer up guys like Spencer. How long was it Spencer?

(Pause.)

Well Spencer? Did you know Spencer was inside Dinger?

DINGER. Aye well…most of em in here have.

MIKE. Crime of passion was it Spencer? Do you reckon Dinger? Go on give us a smile.

SPENCER. I'm, I'm going to my room.

(SPENCER goes to exit.)

MIKE. STAND STILL!

About turn.

(SPENCER obeys. MIKE drops the petty cash box and approaches SPENCER blocking his path to his room.)

Smile. I said smile.

(Pause.)

DINGER. Sorted now Mike, eh?

MIKE. Sooner he smiles sooner we can all be on our way.

(Pause.)

(cajoling) Come on Spencer. Give us a smile. There's a good lad.

(SPENCER attempts to smile.)

Come on let's see that smile. You can do better than that Spencer.

(SPENCER tries harder.)

Oh oh oh, there he is. Turn around. Give us a look. Let Dinger see it.

There we go, that's all I wanted.

(MIKE head butts him in the face. SPENCER drops to his knees holding his face.)

DINGER. Fuck!

(MIKE grabs SPENCER by the hair.)

MIKE. Come on smiler. Off to your room then. Off we go.

(MIKE drags SPENCER by the hair to his room which is just off. SPENCER screams. DINGER is left, he doesn't know what to do. We hear MIKE savagely beating SPENCER who screams. This continues for an uncomfortable length of time. DINGER is paralysed with fear. The beating stops. MIKE enters holding his fist, some blood is visible. He picks up the petty cash box and approaches DINGER.)

Not a word. Ok Dinger? He had that coming. You've got kids Dinger. Dinger?

(Slight Pause.)

You know what he is, don't you? So not a word.

Here.

(MIKE takes a five pound note out of the petty cash box.)

Get yourself a few bottles.

(Pause.)

Well come on.

(Pause.)

Dinger take it.

(DINGER takes the note.)

Not a word. Right? I fucking mean it.

DINGER. Right.

MIKE. Right.

(MIKE exits.)

Scene Nine

*(The office, moments later. **ANDY** is pacing, **MIKE** enters carrying the cash box, he looks pale and tense. **ANDY** jumps about in jubilation. **MIKE** puts the box on the desk.)*

ANDY. *(ecstatic)* Get in! Thank you thank you thank/ you.

MIKE. Shut up.

ANDY. Who had it?

MIKE. I mean it, shut up. Plug that in.

*(**ANDY** puts the plug back in and then opens the cash box.)*

ANDY. Yes. Yes, yesss.

Mike, who had it?

MIKE. Dinger. Dinger had it, shit.

ANDY. Good, Jesus I owe you one.

MIKE. Aye, don't mention it. Fuck!

ANDY. What?

MIKE. Listen, just…

ANDY. What, /what's…?

MIKE. You'll have to, in a minute/ you'll have…

ANDY. What, I'll…what?

MIKE. Spencer's not so good, you'll have/ to…

ANDY. Spencer?

MIKE. You need to ring an ambulance.

ANDY. Ambulance!?

MIKE. No first, first you check, check him and then/ phone.

ANDY. But how has Spencer if Dinger…?

MIKE. Go up and check/ then.

44

(**ANDY** *notices the blood.*)

ANDY. Mike, what have you done?

MIKE. During inquiries… Spencer, he got in the way.

ANDY. Spencer got in the way!?

MIKE. Spencer was…was not cooperating so you…very soon you need to ring an ambulance.

ANDY. Shit, what did…? is it bad? Fuck, what if he says something?

MIKE. He won't. Just, will you just do/ what I…

ANDY. Mike what if/ he…

MIKE. He won't.

ANDY. How do you know?/ I mean…

MIKE. In a minute just go up.

ANDY. Me?

MIKE. Go up and check on him.

ANDY. I'm not… I'm nothing to/ do with…

MIKE. You're gonna say you heard a crash, went up had a look then rang an ambulance. Don't go into the room, right. Just go up open his door, look in, and then ring an ambulance.

ANDY. How bad is it?

MIKE. Ring the ambulance, then go back up put him in the recovery position/ he'll be…

ANDY. Recovery/ position!

MIKE. He'll be away in no time. Been drinking all day, gone to his room, fallen, hit his head.

ANDY. But…

MIKE. Go and do it.

ANDY. Fuck, this is, this/ is…

MIKE. Do it now, and look normal.

ANDY. Did anyone else see, hear anything?

MIKE. No, just Dinger.

ANDY. Dinger!

MIKE. Don't worry. I have an understanding with Dinger.

ANDY. Jesus fuck. They'll want to know why the cameras were off.

MIKE. They won't.

ANDY. Course they will, when he's...

MIKE. There'll be no questions, not with him.

ANDY. But, but...

MIKE. No one'll bother, I guarantee it. No one gives a fuck, they fight, steal from each other, overdose, choke on their vomit. There's no family, police aren't bothered, it doesn't get investigated. Specially with him.

ANDY. But he...

MIKE. He fell and hit his head. And now, right now, you have to go up check then phone an ambulance.

ANDY. They're bound to, you can't just...just well...

MIKE. I've just saved your job, you owe me.

ANDY. I know, I know, just...

MIKE. WILL YOU STOP ACTING LIKE A FUCKING FANNY AND GO AND DO IT!

(ANDY exits. MIKE then looks at CCTV monitor. We see ANDY walk down a corridor, open a door, then rush back down the corridor to the office. ANDY enters panicking.)

ANDY. Fuck Mike... I mean what the fuck?

MIKE. Calm down, make the call, and he'll be out of here in fifteen minutes.

ANDY. He's...he's...

MIKE. End of problem.

ANDY. We are so fucked.

MIKE. Nasty fall.

ANDY. Nasty fall!

(MIKE lifts a cordless phone from the desk and offers it to ANDY.)

Here's the phone.
I, I don't know if I can.

MIKE. You need to phone this second, you're on camera checking. You need to phone right now.

(**MIKE** *dials then listens.*)

It's ringing, here.

(**ANDY** *takes the phone.*)

ANDY. Right, right, ok.

(**ANDY** *puts the phone to his ear.*)

MIKE. I'm nipping out, back in a bit.

(**MIKE** *exits.*)

ANDY. What...?

Sorry hello, ambulance please.

ACT II

Scene One

(The office. **HELEN** *sits at the desk.* **ANDY** *sits at the side reading a Guardian newspaper. There is a knock at the door.)*

HELEN. It's open.

*(***SPENCER** *enters. His face is severely bruised and swollen, his are eyes practically closed. There are stitches on his head which is also bandaged. He has broken ribs which cause him to move with difficulty.)*

Jesus Christ.

*(***SPENCER** *takes money from his pocket and puts it on the desk.)*

SPENCER. Come to pay my rent.

HELEN. *(to* **ANDY***)* Bit of a tumble?

Look at the state of you Spencer. Who's done that?

SPENCER. Fell.

HELEN. What, off the roof?

SPENCER. S'nowt this.

HELEN. Sit down, give me a look.

SPENCER. It's fine.

HELEN. *(to* **ANDY***)* You never said it was this bad?

ANDY. Well yeah, I mean as soon as I saw him, ambulance straight away, I thought I said.

HELEN. Right, so what happened exactly?

48

ANDY. I... I'm not sure, I mean I went up, heard a crash and went up. Spencer was in a bit of a state. Weren't you Spencer? Had a right tumble.

HELEN. Spencer?

SPENCER. What do I owe? Twenty four is it?

HELEN. Sit down Spencer.

Andy will you put that through? And pass us the first aid box.

(**SPENCER** *remains standing.*)

ANDY. Right, yeah.

(**ANDY** *takes the money from* **SPENCER.**)

HELEN. Look at the state of that dressing. You've been picking it. That needs cleaning.

(**ANDY** *gives* **HELEN** *the first aid box and pays the money into a tin and writes a receipt.*)

SPENCER. *(protesting)* No, it's fine, it's alright.

HELEN. It'll get infected. Sit.

(**SPENCER** *sits with difficulty.*)

SPENCER. Na, na... I'm alreet.

HELEN. You'll get a gangrene heed.

(**HELEN** *takes surgical gloves and antiseptic wipes from the first aid box, she puts on the gloves.*)

Sit still.

(**SPENCER** *sits with difficulty.* **HELEN** *removes* **SPENCER**'s *dressing and starts cleaning* **SPENCER**'s *cut with a wipe.* **SPENCER** *winces.*)

Don't be such a big girl's blouse.

(**HELEN** *continues cleaning.*)

What time was this Andy?

ANDY. When?

HELEN. On Thursday, when Spencer did this?

ANDY. It was, when was it? Eight, half eight, maybe nine. Not entirely sure. I heard a crash and went up and, and Spencer was lying on his floor. Must've cracked his head off the sink or... You'd quite a bit to drink hadn't you Spencer?

SPENCER. Yeah.

(HELEN *cleans the wound, throws the dirty wipe in the bin and applies a new dressing.*)

HELEN. Who were you with on Thursday?

ANDY. Umm, Mike.

HELEN. Mike.

(ANDY *finishes writing the receipt.*)

ANDY. There's your receipt Spencer and a pound change. Pleasure doing business with you.

(ANDY *slides the receipt across the desk to* SPENCER.)

SPENCER. Ta.

ANDY. No problemo.

HELEN. Funny, was on training with Mike yesterday, he never mentioned it.

ANDY. No?

HELEN. No.

ANDY. What training?

HELEN. Protecting Vulnerable Adults. He normally likes a good war story Mike, bit of blood and guts. Surprised he didn't mention it.

(*to* SPENCER) How long did they keep you in?

SPENCER. Couple of days.

HELEN. That's some fall. Did you record it in the accident book Andy?

ANDY. No, sorry, I didn't realise.

HELEN. Mike didn't mention it?

ANDY. No, no I don't think he did. It was a busy shift. He must've forgot.

HELEN. Yeah, he must have. I'll show you how to do that later.

ANDY. Ok.

(Pause.)

ANDY. Coffee Helen?

HELEN. No thanks.

ANDY. *(yawns)* Think I might, wake me up a bit. See you later Spencer.

*(**ANDY** gets up, yawns and exits. **HELEN** finishes applying the dressing, she takes off the surgical gloves and throws them in the bin.)*

HELEN. Right, done. Don't pick at it.

*(**SPENCER** gets up.)*

SPENCER. Ta.

*(**SPENCER** goes to exit.)*

HELEN. Spencer?

SPENCER. Aye.

HELEN. Tell us what happened.

SPENCER. I did, fell. Too much drink.

HELEN. I'm not stupid.

SPENCER. It's nowt this.

HELEN. This is your home, you don't have to put up with… no one has the right/ to…

SPENCER. I'm fine.

(Slight Pause.)

Fine.

*(**SPENCER** exits.)*

Scene Two

(End of corridor by a bathroom. MIKE and ANDY stand outside DINGER's bedroom, they wear rubber gloves. A mop leans against a wall. There is a bin bag, air freshener and kitchen tongs on the floor. DINGER enters.)

MIKE. It's happening.

DINGER. Ahh man.

MIKE. Come on.

DINGER. Never.

MIKE. Dinger.

ANDY. You know you want to.

DINGER. I mean it.

MIKE. Watch him Andy, watch him.

ANDY. I'm watching him.

MIKE. You will cooperate ye dirty auld shite…

(DINGER picks up the mop and brandishes it throughout the following. MIKE and ANDY edge closer.)

Watch the exit, don't take your eyes off him for one second.

ANDY. I'm on him.

MIKE. They're coming off. One way or another they're coming off.

DINGER. Molesters! Get back!

MIKE. Ready to take him down?

DINGER. We shall fight on the beaches…

ANDY. Ready.

DINGER. we shall fight in/ the fields…

MIKE. On three.

DINGER. and in the streets.

MIKE. One!

DINGER. We shall fight in the hills.

MIKE. Two!

DINGER. We shall never surrender.

MIKE. Three!

> (**MIKE** *and* **ANDY** *pounce.* **DINGER** *roars and flails wildly.*)

DINGER. NEVER!!

MIKE. Hold him...hold him...

ANDY. I'm...fuck me...

> (**MIKE** *and* **ANDY** *disarm* **DINGER.** **ANDY** *is overcome by the smell and is dry retching.*)

MIKE. Jacket first...get the jacket off...

ANDY. I'm... I'm...uggggh... Jesus...

> (**MIKE** *and* **ANDY** *remove his jacket.*)

DINGER. I'll do it. Get off us. I'll do it.

MIKE. You swear?

DINGER. Swear...just get off...

MIKE. If we let you go and...so/ help me...

DINGER. I'LL GO IN THE FUCKING BATH!

> (**MIKE** *and* **ANDY** *release* **DINGER.**)

> (*gesturing to the mop on the floor*) Watch you don't trip on that.

> (**MIKE** *bends to pick up the mop.* **DINGER** *goes to dodge past him.*)

ANDY. Mike!

> (**MIKE** *blocks* **DINGER**'s *path with the mop and then uses it to prod him into the bathroom.*)

DINGER. Joke joke joke...

MIKE. Go. I've put a rubber duck in.

DINGER. Fuck your duck.

MIKE. Andy, get the stuff.

(ANDY picks up the air freshener, bin bag and kitchen tongs. He sprays air freshener around DINGER's jacket.)

DINGER. Eh! There are natural pheromones.

MIKE. I want all of your clothes out here.

(DINGER exits to the bathroom. ANDY follows him to the door spraying air freshener.)

ANDY. What sort of job is this?

MIKE. I do it for the glamour.

(DINGER's shirt, jeans, then socks are thrown from the bathroom. As each item lands ANDY picks them up with the tongs and puts them in the bag. MIKE furiously mops the area of floor on which the clothes have landed.)

(Pause.)

And the kegs.

(A horrifically soiled pair of y-fronts are thrown from the bathroom.)

ANDY. Holy Christ.

MIKE. Well go on then.

(ANDY blasts the y-fronts with air freshener before putting them in the bag with the tongs.)

(shouting to DINGER) I wanna hear splashing in there.

DINGER. Splish fucking splash.

MIKE. The sound of scrubbing on rancid flesh.

DINGER. *(from off)* Piss off.

(SPENCER enters carrying a bag. He stops in the doorway when he sees MIKE.)

MIKE. Alright Spencer?

(SPENCER stops frozen.)

ANDY. Alright Spencer?

SPENCER. I, uh, bathroom.

MIKE. Dinger's in there. Won't be long.

SPENCER. It's alright.

MIKE. See the auld head's on the mend Spencer.

(MIKE makes a motion towards SPENCER's head. SPENCER jumps and raises his arms to protect himself dropping his bag.)

SPENCER. Get off us.

MIKE. Woah man! Jesus.

(MIKE picks up SPENCER's bag and holds it out to him.)

Take it, take it, here.

(SPENCER takes the bag.)

I'll give you knock when he's finished.

SPENCER. I'm alright.

(SPENCER exits. During the following we hear DINGER bursting into bouts of bath time singing.)

ANDY. Fuck Mike, he's gonna say something.

MIKE. He won't, just.

ANDY. Do you think we should…?

MIKE. What?

ANDY. I don't know, have a word with him.

MIKE. A word?

ANDY. Like, sorry, or…

MIKE. Sorry! No. No way. Maybe.

(Slight Pause.)

No leave him. Stick to the story.

ANDY. This is a fucking nightmare.

MIKE. You're fine. You weren't the one who…

ANDY. Still, I was, what's the word?

MIKE. A fanny.

ANDY. An accessory.

MIKE. It'll be fine.

ANDY. You keep saying fine, this does not feel fucking fine.

MIKE. It will be, I will not, not let this…as long as we just keep saying the same thing then…

ANDY. Dinger knows, I mean anything could come out of his mouth.

MIKE. Keep your voice down.

ANDY. *(quieter)* Sorry.

MIKE. Dinger's not a problem. We can keep Dinger sweet.

ANDY. I mean, Jesus Mike, did you not think, hmm, maybe I should stop now. Now that I can see his fucking skull.

MIKE. Yeah no, no, that's fair, I accept that...but there is no way I am going to let this... I've got a family, I will make sure that this does not become a problem for us.

ANDY. I'm just not the sort of person who's used to... I cried at Watership Down for fuck sake.

MIKE. Right, first of all they were rabbits, he's a kiddy fiddler.

ANDY. Helen suspects something.

MIKE. She doesn't.

ANDY. I'm sure she does. You should've heard her talking to him, all Florence Nightingale.

MIKE. Don't worry about Helen.

ANDY. She's suspicious, I know she is.

MIKE. Leave Helen to me. Anyway, I've an idea when it comes to Helen.

ANDY. What?

MIKE. Think I might have to fuck her again.

(Short Pause.)

ANDY. That's a joke?

MIKE. Well one us should. You game?

ANDY. You're not serious.

MIKE. Think about it.

ANDY. No.

MIKE. It's not the worst idea, you can practically taste the desperation off her.

ANDY. You're mental, you're not well.

MIKE. Just saying.

(Pause.)

ANDY. Do you ever think...?

MIKE. What?

ANDY. Us, I mean, what makes us any better than…?

MIKE. Than him?

ANDY. Not him obviously. But I mean, we come in here, drink when we can get away with it…then drink when you get home, so, only difference, pretty much is we've got the keys.

MIKE. There's a big fucking difference.

ANDY. Is there? I can't remember the last time I'd a solid shit.

MIKE. Yes, a big difference. Don't even fucking begin to… I, I provide for my family, pay taxes, walk the dog. Sometimes I come in, and Karen's been called into the school for the third time in a week…looks suicidal, and it scares me shitless. But I keep going back, I keep coming in here, doing this, for them, and going back, which is more than any of them have ever done.

ANDY. And is that enough?

MIKE. It's got to be, cus at the minute it's taking everything within me to keep that up and not…not…

(Slight Pause.)

You haven't told anyone?

ANDY. No.

MIKE. Your lass?

ANDY. No, Jesus. Guess what we did in work today dear?

MIKE. Not been running around like a fucking headless budgie?

ANDY. No. It's fine honestly, I've been playing it cool.

MIKE. Playing it cool?

(The doorbell rings. ANDY jumps.)

For fuck sake.

ANDY. I'll go.

MIKE. It'll be Helen. Sure you're not tempted?

ANDY. Not funny.

Scene Three

(The lounge. ANDY is dozing on a chair, there are playing cards on the table. SPENCER knocks then enters. ANDY snores. SPENCER clears his throat. ANDY keeps snoring. SPENCER clears his throat louder. No response from ANDY.)

SPENCER. Andy.

(No response from ANDY. SPENCER shakes ANDY's shoulder, he wakes suddenly.)

ANDY. Wha... Spence what are you doing? You can't come in here.

SPENCER. Here.

(SPENCER holds out a bunch of keys.)

Here.

ANDY. Shit, where were they?

SPENCER. You left them.

ANDY. Thanks Spencer.

SPENCER. In the door, of the meds room. Anyone could've...

ANDY. Cheers Spencer, you're a life saver.

SPENCER. S'alright.

ANDY. I owe you one. Here, here.

(ANDY takes a packet of cigarettes out of his pocket and offers them to SPENCER.)

SPENCER. I'm alright.

ANDY. Go on, take them.

(SPENCER takes the cigarettes.)

SPENCER. Ta.

(Pause.)

Not like him.

ANDY. What?

SPENCER. The other one. Done this.

*(**SPENCER** touches the cut on his head.)*

ANDY. I don't, I'm not sure what you mean.

SPENCER. Think you do.

ANDY. No.

SPENCER. No?

*(**MIKE** enters.)*

MIKE. What are you doing Spencer?

SPENCER. I just...his keys, he...

ANDY. He found my keys.

MIKE. Found your fucking keys!

Back to your room Spencer.

*(**SPENCER** goes to exit and stops at the door.)*

SPENCER. Thanks for the tabs.

*(**SPENCER** exits.)*

MIKE. Thanks for the tabs!

ANDY. He found my keys, I'd left them out there.

MIKE. You gave him a fucking tabs!

ANDY. I'd left them in the meds room door...anyone could've...so, I'd fallen asleep, I wasn't awake.

MIKE. Was it a degree in art history you said you cocked up?

ANDY. Yeah.

MIKE. You should've studied being a bell end. You'd've passed that with flying colours you dozy cunt. And don't try to get all paly.

ANDY. I'm not, I just...he brought my keys back.

MIKE. Watch yourself.

(MIKE takes a bottle of cider from the filing cabinet and fills both mugs on the table.)

See mother of the year's back. What did I tell you? Didn't last a week.

ANDY. Yeah. She's in some state.

MIKE. Now her, her I feel sorry for. Still, she should be sterilised. That kid'll be a mess, doesn't stand a chance.

ANDY. If it gets put in a good home, might be all right.

MIKE. Na, look at the pregnancy, think about the shit going into her body. And her screaming, angry all the time, with it inside her, while it's growing. That's only gonna end up one way. It is fucked.

ANDY. You're saying it should just be written off? From day one, from birth.

MIKE. I guarantee that kid'll be locked up or in somewhere like this by the time it's eighteen.

ANDY. Maybe.

(Slight Pause.)

Your deal.

MIKE. Aye right.

(MIKE deals cards they drink and stare at their cards in silence.)

Not a bad number this, is it?

ANDY. What?

MIKE. Getting paid to drink and play cards. Beats working for a living. How old are you?

ANDY. Twenty three.

MIKE. Twenty three, I'd been halfway round the world by then. Mainly hell holes.

ANDY. Can't have been more of a hell hole than this.

MIKE. This? A hell hole? This Disney on Ice. This is Club Tropicana with a cherry on top.

ANDY. You reckon?

MIKE. What was I doing at your age? South Armagh. Ah the joys, one false move there and you'd had it, simple as. Did I tell you what they done to my mate Rod?

ANDY. No. But I think you're going to.

(Slight Pause.)

MIKE. Now Rod, Rod was a half wit. Nice kid, would give you owt. But essentially had the brains of a potato waffle. We convinced him it took thirty baby duffles to make a duffle coat.

ANDY. Seriously?

MIKE. Seriously. He vanished from a pub car park, he was just gone a few minutes. Chasing skirt. We knew, searched for a few days, checked this disused timber yard. I walk into a barn and the fucker's stood there. Just standing at the back of this barn. I go up, calling him all the twats under the sun...and...it's not till... I was as far as I am form you now. I've gone right up talking to him, and not seen that there's, there's a drill bit...a drill bit's been put through his forehead and into the wall behind. That's what was holding him up. I was talking to him and...

(Pause.)

Right through his head.

ANDY. Jesus.

MIKE. That wasn't the worst thing they done to him, not by long way. He would have been relieved when that went in.

(Pause.)

ANDY. What else had?

MIKE. You don't want to know.

ANDY. Right.

MIKE. Pick axe handle, hammered inside him. Up his hole all the way.

(Slight Pause.)

So this is Butlins. What we used to do after that, this was
fun. We'd pull a suspect, take em up in a helicopter.
Batter them first obviously. We'd fly them about for a
bit, hang them out over the side. They'd be screaming.
And we'd get a hood on them. Have them out over the
edge. Begging. But then we'd go down low. They'd no
idea, but we're just five, six foot off the ground. And
they're screaming, fucking howling. And we'd be like,
this is it Paddy, this is fucking it you bog monkey. Then
we'd let go of them, let them drop. Fucking hilarious.
Dropped one on a dead cow once.

If I'd the chance to…catch the bastards that did that
to him.

(Pause.)

I'd to hold his head still while someone cut through
the drill bit with a hacksaw.

It's probably not everyone's cup of tea.

ANDY. No.

MIKE. Definitely not for everyone. Queen and country, all
that. Pile of shite. One of Thatcher's henchmen, that's
all we were. But the money was alright and there was
fuck all else happening round here at the time. Unless
you fancied being a polis so you could batter miners
and kill fucking football fans.

ANDY. Not exactly much happening round here now, but…

MIKE. And what is it you wanna be doing now, given the
choice?

ANDY. I dunno.

MIKE. If I'd been to university I'd want to know. You should
ask for your money back.

ANDY. I umm, it's stupid really.

MIKE. What?

ANDY. I quite fancied being a curator.

MIKE. A curator! What, hanging pictures up and that?

ANDY. It's not just…anyway it's not likely, so…

MIKE. And how does one become a curator?

ANDY. Yeah exactly, don't know what I was thinking.

MIKE. No you go for it. If there's one thing everyone's after in times of economic crisis, it's someone to come round and hang their pictures up nice.

ANDY. I know, quite frankly I'm getting sick of the Guggenheim ringing me up every day going, please will you come over and hang our pictures up nice.

MIKE. Well until you get the offer that's right for you, you're best sticking it out in here.

(They both drink.)

What you got?

ANDY. Three of a kind.

*(**MIKE** places his cards down one by one.)*

MIKE. Read em and weep, a flush which is quite apt cos that means you dear boy are on toilet duty.

ANDY. Bollocks.

MIKE. There's a particularly artistic arrangement of bloody vomit with a syringe in it in the downstairs bathroom. Perhaps you could do something nice with that.

*(From off we hear **DINGER** approaching singing.)*

Here he comes.

*(**MIKE** shouts to the door.)*

What do you want?

*(**DINGER** enters, he is very drunk. He notices the bottle and gestures towards it.)*

DINGER. Ahh…a little sup/ perhaps…

MIKE. Get away from that you dirty bastard. What are you after?

DINGER. De de… I came…dumps.

MIKE. Dumps.

DINGER. If you would be so kind.

MIKE. Work away.

(**DINGER** *bends over the ashtray on the table picks out
the cigarette butts. His progress is tortuously slow.*)

MIKE. Living the dream, eh Dinger?

DINGER. Living the dream Michael, living the...

(Pause.)

How has...

(**DINGER** *takes his tobacco tin form his pocket and
drops the cigarette butts in it. He stands swaying for a
moment.*)

ANDY. You alright Dinger?

DINGER. How has this...at when. Look at this, how has it
come to this?

MIKE. Easily done, easy as falling off a bike.

DINGER. Correct. Chips! I went out for chips. Out for chips
then...think it was chips.

(**DINGER** *belches then smells it.*)

That's chips.

Couldn't tell ye exactly when. But then...well got to
divint ye.

ANDY. Got to what?

DINGER. Sup, but social, very social, just a wee...ooh don't
mind if I do, to be social. Too fucking social, that was
my problem.

(**DINGER** *staggers.*)

ANDY. *(to **MIKE**)* Do you reckon we should...?

DINGER. Then, the next thing...you're being social by
yourself, extremely...very social, just you yourself. And
the, all them... Ronnie, Wingnut, the bunch of cunts
you do the socialising with, they're...they're, they see
you coming and shooo, other side of the street. Locks
getting changed when you're out. I, I remember that
one. Do you know, diving through a patio window, it's
not...not half as easy you'd imagine. Scares the bairns
as well apparently...so she said.

(Pause.)

Goats man.

ANDY. Goats?

(DINGER bleats.)

Think he's lost it Mike, gone.

MIKE. This is good, wait'll ye hear.

DINGER. Afghan goats, them's the best. Couldn't tell ye how I came to be sleeping with em…not a, not a clue. That to this day remains a mystery.

ANDY. What?

(DINGER bleats which causes a small coughing fit. A string of slabber hangs from his mouth which he catches in his hand and wipes on his jacket.)

MIKE. Lovely.

Have you not heard where Dinger was residing before here?

ANDY. No.

DINGER. Kipping with the goats… Afghans, Afghan goats, I'm not prejudice, down pets corner. Ye hear…in here…all the time ye hear em, dozy bastards. Should send all the pakis back, and all that…that fuckin bollocks. Not me, I'm all for it, you get quite a bit of heat off an Afghan mountain goat, it's not too bad… not too bad at all. Apart from the smell.

MIKE. I'm sure the goats got used to it.

(MIKE and ANDY laugh.)

DINGER. I'd have probably froze. Nah, I'm all for them coming over here. More the merrier as far as I'm concerned.

D'ye know, d'ye know what he said to me?

MIKE. Who?

DINGER. That…that inbred Mackem.

MIKE. Reggie.

DINGER. That's the one. This was today, today Reggie tried to explain to me that we are a genetically superior race.

(DINGER laughs.)

This is a Mackem.

(All laugh.)

I'm not shitting ye, Reggie was, he was sat there, trying to tell me, that genetically it had been proved, proved by scientists, that white people were more ad...ad... more better...more advanced. And he knew this, cus he'd read all about it in a leaflet.

(Slight Pause.)

I couldn't believe it.

(Pause.)

Couldn't believe he could fucking read for a start.

(MIKE and ANDY laugh. DINGER continues now enjoying himself.)

Listen...listen now...the best bit...as he was telling me this, he was...while...while he was telling me about his genetical superiority...as he was doing that he was drinking a bottle of aftershave, that he'd stole from Poundland.

(All laugh.)

(still laughing) And he offered me a swig of his aftershave, and I looked at it. It was fucking alcohol free.

(All laugh.)

So...so there's your master race, right there. We are superior beings.

(Laughter subsides. Long Pause.)

I'm gonna stop. And, and I mean that.

(DINGER takes a photograph from his jacket.)

You seen my Bruce Mike?

MIKE. You've shown us, aye.

(DINGER gives the picture to ANDY. ANDY studies it for a moment.)

ANDY. Looks like you. Do ye see much of him?

DINGER. Na. The youngest, Rebecca, I've nowt, no picture...nothing. And I wouldn't, if I saw her now... she could pass, walk past me in the street, and I wouldn't know...my little girl.

(DINGER breaks down.)

I am going to stop.

MIKE. Here.

(MIKE hands him a cigarette.)

DINGER. Much obliged.

(ANDY gets up hands him back the photograph. DINGER puts it in his jacket.)

ANDY. Come on.

(ANDY helps DINGER to exit.)

MIKE. Gonna stop.

Scene Four

(Corridor. **KERRY** *enters staggering, barely keeping herself up. She tries a door which is locked.)*

KERRY. Bastards.

*(***KERRY*** half drops her bottoms and starts to urinate on the floor. During this she topples over and remains motionless for a moment. She then rolls around attempting to pull her bottoms up and get up, groaning as she does so. She fails and gives up, lies still and her eyes drop shut.* **ANDY** *enters.)*

ANDY. Kerry. Kerry.

*(***ANDY*** stands and looks at* **KERRY.** *He is reluctant to get too close.)*

Come on Kerry, up you get.

*(***ANDY*** looks up and down the corridor. He walks away from her and shouts.)*

MIKE. MIKE COULD YOU COME HERE A SECOND?

*(***MIKE*** enters.)*

MIKE. Ah for fuck sake.

*(***MIKE*** kneels next to* **KERRY.***)*

Lets get them up.

*(***MIKE*** pulls up her bottoms in one swift movement. He puts his head close to hers and listens to her breathing.)*

Shit, right Kerry.

*(***MIKE*** puts her in the recovery position. He puts two fingers in her mouth and moves her tongue from blocking her airway. He squeezes her shoulder.)*

Kerry! Kerry!

(**KERRY** *coughs.* **MIKE** *smells his hands and winces.*)

Charming.

KERRY. *(struggling to catch her breath)* Uggh God.

MIKE. Can't be lying out here Kerry.

KERRY. I'm alright.

MIKE. I beg to differ. Need to get you your room.

KERRY. You got a tab?

MIKE. No. Soup or toad in the hole?

KERRY. What?

MIKE. I imagine soup would go down easier.

KERRY. I'm not eatin.

MIKE. It wasn't a question.

KERRY. I mean it.

MIKE. So do I. You're having something if I've to force it down you myself.

KERRY. What sort of soup?

MIKE. Tomato.

KERRY. Don't give us much.

MIKE. You'll need to get a wash as well.

KERRY. Aye, I know.

MIKE. Andy get Kerry a clean towel will you.

ANDY. Yeah.

KERRY. Thanks

MIKE. Right Kerry. Need to get you on your feet. Here we go. Get your feet underneath you, there's a good girl. On three. One, two, three.

(**MIKE** *supports* **KERRY** *to her feet. She is all over the place.*)

MIKE. Get your legs underneath you, there's a good girl. Right, off to your room then and I'll bring your soup in.

(**MIKE** *supports* **KERRY** *to the exit.*)

MIKE. Oh Andy, could you clear that piss up, cheers mate.

(**MIKE** *and* **KERRY** *exit.*)

Scene Five

(The office. **DINGER** *and* **HELEN** *sit at the desk.* **HELEN** *writes on a key working form)*

HELEN. Mr Bell promises he will not return to Bede's World in the foreseeable future.

DINGER. She needs me Helen, she just doesn't realise it yet.

HELEN. Funny way of showing it. How many times has she had you arrested now?

DINGER. Two or three.

HELEN. Nine.

DINGER. You should see her though, words fail me. She's like that domestic goddess wife off the telly, expanded in all the best places and with a come to bed limp. We're made for each other, she's my salvation.

HELEN. There's a fine line between courtship and harassment Dinger.

DINGER. She'll crumble soon enough. Playing hard to get.

HELEN. But you can't go back there. Are we agreed?

DINGER. Aye.

HELEN. Sign there.

*(***HELEN*** passes* **DINGER** *the form and he signs.)*

DINGER. The Vulnerable Bede. What a twat. If he thinks he's vulnerable he should try kipping in a petting zoo in November.

*(***DINGER*** gets up but doesn't exit. Pause.)*

HELEN. Is there anything else I can do for you?

DINGER. No, not really.

HELEN. Well come on spit it out.

DINGER. Naw, it's alreet.

HELEN. Come on Dinger, what is it?

DINGER. Nowt, just…

HELEN. Uh huh.

DINGER. Just it, it wasn't right.

HELEN. What?

DINGER. What happened with…it were my fault.

HELEN. Do you mean Spencer?

DINGER. Aye that. It were me who took the cash box, so
I don't know why he…well I do but…I was just messin
on, but he…

HELEN. Mike? It was Mike wasn't it?

(Pause.)

Dinger?

DINGER. I wrote it down here.

*(**DINGER** takes a folded piece of paper from his jacket
pocket.)*

Na, forget/ it.

HELEN. Dinger you've/ got…

DINGER. Na doesn't…canit spell owt anyways.

*(**DINGER** goes to put the note back in his pocket and goes
to exit. **HELEN** stops him.)*

Na.

HELEN. Please, look. No one needs to know this came from
you.

DINGER. He'll work it out.

HELEN. No, no, the whole thing, it's…it's suspicious,
there's all sorts of things that could…

DINGER. I've never been a grass. Cos at the time I said…
promised I wouldn't…and he paid us.

HELEN. He what?

DINGER. Nowt.

HELEN. How much?

DINGER. Fiver.

HELEN. A fucking fiver!

DINGER. Don't say.

HELEN. I won't.

DINGER. Promise.

HELEN. I promise no one'll find out.

A fiver!

DINGER. I'm not sure Helen. Don't see the point now.

(DINGER *holds out the note and* HELEN *takes it.* ANDY *enters.* HELEN *quickly puts the note in her pocket.*)

ANDY. Morning, sorry I'm late. Alright Dinger?

(ANDY *sits by the desk.*)

DINGER. Champion. Aye cheers Helen.

HELEN. Remember, no more trips to Bede's World.

DINGER. Right.

(DINGER *exits.*)

ANDY. What was he after?

HELEN. Key working session. You look like you slept in a hedge.

ANDY. This fucking place. A year ago I was doing my dissertation on the influence of Japanese woodprints on the French Impressionists. Now, I'm drinking cider that I've taken from a dead man's room at three in the morning, and betting on topless darts. How? I honestly thought, that I might...in some way, be able to do something to help them, or at least, I don't know... how do you end up such a fucking mess?

HELEN. You've got to face facts, don't you? This is my lot, I'm a lonely, fairly rough middle aged woman and I work as a tramp farmer.

ANDY. But that's not just it, is it? I mean there's a lot more than what you look like and what you do. Not that you look...

HELEN. Last week, I was wiping tables in the dining room, and Brendan grabbed my arse.

ANDY. Brendan?!

HELEN. Brendan.

ANDY. Bastard, you didn't say.

HELEN. Yeah, I was wiping the tables in the dining room, and he just grabbed my arse, gave it a squeeze. Didn't say anything.

ANDY. What did you do? He should be out for that.

HELEN. Thing is… I was, for a moment I was a bit flattered. I mean, how tragic is that? A man who's generally too pissed to locate his mouth with a sausage roll grabs my arse, and that boosts my confidence.

ANDY. Shit. Umm, you umm, I don't know…there's the internet dating. You get…there's loads doing that. It's normal, I know loads of…not just weirdo's, everyone's on that now. It's normal…and didn't Mike, no…

(**ANDY** *realises he's put his foot in it.*)

What was I saying?

HELEN. You were going to say, didn't Mike give me one after the Christmas party. Of course he's told you the gory details.

ANDY. No, I don't think…did he? Maybe he mentioned in passing.

HELEN. There is so much disgusts me about that man. So why in the name of Christ do I…? I let him…have no ability to say no…

ANDY. It wasn't just…?

HELEN. Mondays and Thursdays for the past month.

ANDY. He never mentioned that like.

HELEN. While his son's in judo. Handy I'm round the corner from the leisure centre.

ANDY. Oh.

(*Slight Pause.*)

Louise has split up with me.

HELEN. Has she?

ANDY. Yep.

HELEN. Shit sorry Andy, I didn't know.

ANDY. Don't tell Mike.

HELEN. No, I won't.

ANDY. Think he'd be round every night of the week if he knew she'd moved out.

HELEN. When did you split?

ANDY. Last week. She's moved in with Genevieve and Rachael in Walker. They make funky knit ware and sell it on a stall. Louise's got heavily into it, says she finds it therapeutic.

HELEN. Is this definitely it?

ANDY. How do you compete with a household of militant knitters? They're building their own jurt.

HELEN. In Walker!

(**HELEN** *laughs.*)

Sorry Andy. Are you alright?

ANDY. We want different things apparently. But it's done now. Doesn't mean I'm just going to stop and... I've got a job, which is something. Alright, it's a pile of shite. But at the same time, I've got a job which keeps a roof over my head, I'm not destitute just yet.

HELEN. Do not settle for this. Can we make a deal?

ANDY. What?

HELEN. Promise me that you're out of here by Christmas.

ANDY. Yeah, but to do what? I was signing on for months before this.

HELEN. Anything, doesn't matter.

ANDY. And what about your escape?

HELEN. I'll think of something.

Scene Six

(The office. **SPENCER** *stands by the desk.* **MIKE** *enters.)*

MIKE. Sit down.

*(***SPENCER** *sits.* **MIKE** *opens a file and sits opposite him. He takes his time over writing on a form.)*

So, how are you?

SPENCER. Alreet.

MIKE. Alreet! Wonderful. I shall write that in my key worker recording form.

*(***MIKE** *writes on the form.)*

Spencer states that things are, open speech marks, alreet, close speech marks.

Now, what we gonna talk about next? So we've established that things are, alreet. Let's try and flesh that out a bit, for my form here. Let's sex up this document. I know, let's talk about your drinking.

SPENCER. What? What about...

MIKE. You seem to have been hitting the sauce pretty hard lately. Any particular reason for that?

SPENCER. No.

MIKE. Just been in the party spirit have you? Up there in your room. Every day's a party in room Q eh?

(Pause.)

You don't think your drinking's becoming a problem do you Spencer? Cos it'd be terrible if all this drinking had an adverse effect on license, eh? There's loads of agencies we could refer you to. Well? Some do acupuncture.

SPENCER. Na, I'm alright.

MIKE. Super. So on my form, what I'm going to put is. At present Spencer does not wish to receive, I before e, any support with his use of alcohol.

We're fucking flying now aren't we? Now, what next, let's have a think. Hmm.

Oh yeah. I had a nice chat with your probation officer this afternoon. She's lovely, isn't she? Cracking arse, eh Spencer? Wouldn't you say she's got a cracking arse?

(Slight Pause.)

Sorry, I forgot, probably not your type, bit old. Anyway, she was saying that you didn't attend your last group meeting and that you are uncommunicative when you can be arsed to turn up. Now that is very naughty of you Spencer.

SPENCER. Been ill.

MIKE. Have you? Sorry Spencer, I didn't realise. What's been the matter? Have you been to the doctor's?

SPENCER. Just been bad.

MIKE. Just been bad. Not too bad to go to the shop everyday for a bottle or two? Eh? I don't really think you've been that bad, have you Spencer?

(Pause.)

(raising his voice) I said, I don't really think you've been that bad, have you Spencer?

SPENCER. Suppose.

MIKE. You see Spencer, how it looks, when you can't be arsed to turn up to your sessions, it looks like you don't want to be rehabilitated. Doesn't it? And if you don't want to be rehabilitated, it makes me think, that you think, you haven't done anything wrong. Is that right Spencer? Do you think that you haven't done anything wrong?

(Slight Pause.)

Well? Do you think you've done nothing wrong?

(Pause.)

(MIKE jumps up throws his chair to the ground. SPENCER dives to the floor and cowers protecting his head.)

ANSWER THE FUCKING QUESTION!

SPENCER. No. Don't…please…

MIKE. NO! No what? I've done nothing wrong, not a thing.

SPENCER. I have, I have. I'm…

(SPENCER is terrified and shaking.)

MIKE. Good, well glad we got to the bottom that. So you're going to go to the sessions then aren't you?

SPENCER. Yes.

(MIKE picks his chair up and sits back down at the desk.)

MIKE. Not going to miss anymore, to make sure that nothing like that ever happens again? You fucking disgusting piece of shit.

SPENCER. I'll go I'll go.

MIKE. Sign it.

(MIKE pushes the form and pen across the desk. SPENCER gets up. As SPENCER approaches MIKE scares him causing him to jump. MIKE laughs while SPENCER signs. HELEN enters.)

Just been doing a spot of the old key working with our Spencer here.

HELEN. So I heard.

MIKE. Spencer has been a very naughty boy. He skipped one of his nonce club sessions at probation.

HELEN. Mike.

You get yourself away if you're done then Spencer.

SPENCER. Thank you.

(SPENCER exits.)

HELEN. Very big of you, I must say.

MIKE. Are you defending him?

HELEN. In this instance, yes, yes I am defending him.

MIKE. Have you got kids? No. Well when, if you do, then come and tell me we should all just forgive and forget and have a lovely big group hug.

HELEN. I know it was you.

MIKE. Know it was me what?

HELEN. Spencer's fall.

(Pause.)

MIKE. Big fucking deal.

HELEN. It is actually.

MIKE. Have you heard yourself? The things he's done, and he's allowed to walk/ about like…

HELEN. Right, asides from that. You were on with Andy.

MIKE. It was his fucking mess/ that…

HELEN. That would wreck his future, involved in something like that.

MIKE. Nothing's come of it, no witnesses, it's fine.

HELEN. You think so?

MIKE. Are you…?

HELEN. What?

MIKE. Threatening, threatening to…

HELEN. No, of course not.

MIKE. Then I could do without this shit.

HELEN. Did you not stop to think?

MIKE. Yes, that's exactly what I did. I thought I have chance to hurt this fucker that's wrecked lives. And I'd do it again in the same situation.

HELEN. And what about Andy's life, if it came out? And yours for that matter, you'd be a lot of use to your family in jail.

MIKE. You'd love that wouldn't you?

HELEN. What?

MIKE. Have me locked away, bet you're tempted.

HELEN. No I wouldn't actually.

MIKE. Can't stand it can you?

HELEN. Grow up Mike.

MIKE. Can't stand the idea of me.

(*HELEN turns away.*)

HELEN. Yeah, you're probably onto something there like.

MIKE. But that's your problem isn't it? Cos at the same time...

HELEN. Don't.

MIKE. At the same time, we both know, that you fucking love it.

(*MIKE stands close behind HELEN and talks into her ear.*)

Isn't that right Helen?

(*MIKE reaches around her and holds her breasts.*)

HELEN. Don't, please.

MIKE. Isn't it though?

(*MIKE rubs her breasts.*)

HELEN. No...

MIKE. You want it and you can't stand it.

HELEN. Stop.

(*MIKE continues. HELEN appears frozen.*)

MIKE. Hate the fact that...

HELEN. Please, will you...

MIKE. that the hands that beat the fuck out of that sick bastard are touching you...

HELEN. Mike.

MIKE. and you like it don't you?

HELEN. I want you to stop.

MIKE. No you don't.

HELEN. Stop.

MIKE. I can feel you don't.

HELEN. Not here.

MIKE. Why not?

HELEN. No…not…

(**MIKE** *rubs his hips against* **HELEN** *and reaches between her legs.*)

MIKE. Come on.

HELEN. Can't, here…

MIKE. Why not?

HELEN. No.

MIKE. Just a quick one.

HELEN. God.

(*Banging on the office door.* **MIKE** *releases* **HELEN.**)

MIKE. Fuck sake.

WE'RE CLOSED.

DINGER. (*from off*) Bungle's stood with his cock out in the empty bath again, and I'm busting for a shite.

MIKE. Brilliant.

Scene Seven

(Office. **HELEN** *is sitting at the desk.* **KERRY** *enters.)*

KERRY. Will you do us some cheese on toast?

HELEN. Kitchen's shut now Kerry.

KERRY. Aw fuck off. Please.

HELEN. It's half eleven.

KERRY. Please Helen, I'm starving.

HELEN. There's bread and a toaster out there on the side.

KERRY. Wouldn't dare touch that.

HELEN. Would you not?

KERRY. With these manky bastards.

HELEN. Better than that are you?

(Short Pause.)

KERRY. You can fuck off. Fuck right off.

HELEN. Out of the office please.

KERRY. Like that now is it?

HELEN. Same rules for everyone pet.

KERRY. Just like the rest of em aren't ye?

HELEN. Go on, off you go.

KERRY. In fact you're worse. Least they didn't try to hide
the fact they're cunts. What the fuck are you? Did
I not live up to your expectations? Have I let you
down? Is that it? What? Were you hoping I'd make you
Godmother? You sad bitch. Bet you did and all. Well
fucking sorry/ about that.

HELEN. Out now or I'm/ calling...

KERRY. Still, least now you can look down your nose at me
with the rest of the arseholes. Shake your head and...
what is it youse say? We've done so much for her, but

81

she just won't help herself. You couldn't give a fuck whether I help myself or not.

HELEN. That's not true.

KERRY. Get me a shitty dressing gown from Primark and I'm meant to jump for joy and live happily ever after.

HELEN. No/ Kerry…

KERRY. Just so you can congratulate yourself on what a wonderful fucking job you're doing. Well I'm sorry, but this. This here, this is me. This is what I am. Suckin off six pakis for a bag of shite gear. And no amount of fucking cuddles or support plans is gonna change it.

(Slight Pause.)

Thought you were gonna visit me anyway?

HELEN. I'm sorry Kerry, I…

KERRY. Don't be sorry for fuck sake. What you sorry for? You think if you'd've come waltzing in with some grapes it all would've worked out differently? I'd be bouncing him on my knee by the fire. You'd be knitting booties. Hate to break it to you, was never gonna happen.

HELEN. Kerry I'm, I'm…please don't, because of this, don't think that things are over for you. Kerry/ you've got…

KERRY. Over for me! Things never fucking started for me. Suppose you think that I'm sat here grieving my loss. Crying myself to sleep.

HELEN. You don't mean/ that.

KERRY. Don't you fucking tell me what I mean.

HELEN. Kerry.

KERRY. This bond, this precious bond I'm meant to…rip it out, take it away, so fuck.

HELEN. Kerry look…

KERRY. I feel nothing. Nothing right.

HELEN. Fine Kerry. You don't care, so neither do I. Like I said, kitchen's shut.

KERRY. Aye, you're right there. I don't care, I do not care one little bit.

HELEN. Alright Kerry, off you go, don't be stupid.

(KERRY slams the desk up and down.)

KERRY. Don't be stupid, sure I am stupid, do stupid things all the time me, one stupid fucking thing after the next.

HELEN. Kerry…. come on…

KERRY. What?

(KERRY continues banging.)

HELEN. I'll do some toast if that's…

KERRY. Aye, you do that.

HELEN. Right off you go, I'll just be/ a…

KERRY. Now.

HELEN. Come on Kerry, off you go.

KERRY. DO IT NOW!

*(KERRY smashes a mug and lunges for **HELEN**. **MIKE** enters quickly and expertly holds **KERRY** in a restraint. She struggles but is held fast.)*

(screaming) GET OFF. I, I'LL FUCKING… MIKE GET OFF NOW!

MIKE. Calm down Kerry, ok, calm down, nice and relaxed.

KERRY. I MEAN IT I'LL…

*(KERRY spits at **HELEN**.)*

MIKE. Calm yourself.

KERRY. GET…

*(KERRY increases the ferocity of her struggling with no effect. **MIKE** waits until she has tired herself out and is out of breath.)*

MIKE. Finished? Deep breaths, nice and relaxed.

(KERRY pants.)

Right Kerry, what's gonna happen next is, I will take you to your room. If you come out again tonight you'll be arrested, and will not set foot in here again. Now you don't want that. Ok?

(Slight Pause.)

Ok?

KERRY. Ok.

MIKE. Right then. Helen.

*(**HELEN** opens the door)*

Off we go. Nice and slowly.

(If there are pieces of broken mug on their path) Watch your feet.

*(**MIKE** takes **KERRY** from the office still in the restraint hold. **KERRY** now puts up no resistance. **HELEN** locks the door.)*

Scene Nine

*(A corridor. **ANDY** is mopping around **DINGER** who is in a heap on the floor. **ANDY** is drunk and staggering.)*

ANDY. Dinger. Dinger.

(No response.)

Dinger.

*(**ANDY** flicks the mop at him. No response.)*

Dinger. Get up.

*(**ANDY** prods him with the mop.)*

Get up ye smelly bastard.

(Pause.)

Look not tonight, please…

*(**ANDY** prods him with the mop. Starting to lose his temper.)*

Fuck sake, will you just…

*(**ANDY** prods him with the mop.)*

You stinking…will you just…look at the state of you… look at the fucking state of you.

*(**ANDY** prods him harder with the mop.)*

Come on, will you just…for once.

What's the point? What's the fucking point of you? You're just…just. Look at you, look at the state of you. Disgusting auld fuck…lying there…lying in piss, shit… fucking stinking.

(Pause.)

You've got kids. Your kids are…and here's their Dad.
Good auld Dinger.

(**ANDY** *flicks him in the face with the mop.*)

Get up.

(*Pause.*)

And you're mister fucking popular in here. Fucking
hell. I, I may be… I…at least when I walk out that door
in five hours time I've got, I've got… I'd be missed. I'd
be missed.

(**ANDY** *flicks him in the face with the mop.*)

There's not a single person'd give a flying fuck if you
never got up from there again.

(**ANDY** *flicks him in the face with the mop.*)

Get in your room.

(**ANDY** *flicks him harder in the face.*)

Go on ye useless bastard.

(**ANDY** *prods him hard in the ribs with the mop.*)

Get up.

(**ANDY** *bends over and shouts.*)

GET UP.

(**ANDY** *pushes the mop down hard on his head and
shouts.*)

GET TO YOUR FUCKING ROOM.

(**ANDY** *gives a series of very hard stabs at* **DINGER** *with
the mop.* **DINGER** *groans and writhes about trying to
escape the blows.* **ANDY** *stops, drops the mop and walks
away. He presses his forehead against the wall and
breathes heavily.* **DINGER** *curls in a ball.*)

Fuck sake.

(**ANDY** *walks back to* **DINGER** *and stands over him.*)

Dinger. Dinger come on mate, sorry. Come on. Dinger.

(Pause.)

Come on to your room Dinger.

*(**ANDY** shakes him.)*

Come on Dinger, let's go.

(Pause.)

You can't just…just stop, just stop living. You've got a brain for fuck sake. When do you decide to just stop?

*(**MIKE** enters.)*

MIKE. You done yet? Chop chop.

ANDY. Give us a hand with him.

MIKE. Just mop round him.

ANDY. Won't take a minute.

MIKE. We've Saw IV to watch. Anyway, company policy.

ANDY. For once, for once can we just do something?

MIKE. Don't see what difference it makes.

ANDY. No, I know you don't, but could we not do it anyway.

MIKE. What's got into you?

ANDY. I just thought that, that before we sit down to watch mindless shit all night we/ could…

MIKE. I've got Snakes On A Plane if…

ANDY. Maybe we could just try to… I just thought for once maybe we could do something, just a small fucking thing.

MIKE. Well if it's gonna make you feel better about yourself.

ANDY. Cos that's such a bad thing is it?

MIKE. Alright, Jesus. Divint pop a nail.

ANDY. Get the other side of him them.

MIKE. Alright Dinger, on three. One, two, three.

*(They raise **DINGER** from under either shoulder and support him off.)*

Scene Ten

(KERRY's room. KERRY sits on the floor in front of her bed. She is heavily intoxicated. She drinks from a bottle of vodka. DINGER knocks then enters.)

DINGER. Enough of that.

(DINGER takes hold of the bottle.)

KERRY. Fuck sake.

DINGER. Enough.

(DINGER takes the bottle and struggles to pull it from KERRY. He sets the bottle out of KERRY's reach.)

KERRY. Give it.

DINGER. No.

KERRY. Give us that here.

DINGER. Enough. You've had enough.

KERRY. Sending me te…

DINGER. Ssshh now…

KERRY. I'm going back out.

(KERRY makes a useless attempt to get up. DINGER easily keeps her down with an arm on her shoulder.)

DINGER. They'll have ye lifted.

KERRY. So fuck, what do I care?

DINGER. You're seein the bairn tomorra?

(Pause.)

KERRY. Stuck up fuckin sluts.

DINGER. Who?

KERRY. WI their looks…looking at us like…like I was…

DINGER. Who's this now?

KERRY. In there.

DINGER. Where?

KERRY. Nurses.

DINGER. Don't bother with that now.

KERRY. Rest all chattin away and…

DINGER. Stop.

KERRY. Pulled the curtain round on me.

DINGER. Don't.

KERRY. Just mine. Rest of em chatting away…havin photos took.

DINGER. Rest yourself.

KERRY. I get the fuckin curtain round on me.

DINGER. Bed time now.

KERRY. Like when they shoot the fallers at the Grand National.

(**KERRY** *sobs and reaches for the bottle.*)

DINGER. No…no, no…

KERRY. Please.

DINGER. Alreet, alreet, here.

(**DINGER** *passes it to her and* **KERRY** *drinks.*)

You cannot keep at this.

KERRY. Aye and your one te…look at you.

DINGER. Exactly, exactly, look at me. You're a young lass.

KERRY. Shite I'm young. This, this is not young.

(*Long pause.*)

DINGER. You've time, you've got time to get this beat. Get this shite beat, you've got to, then there's a chance ye can…be no stoppin ye then.

KERRY. No stoppin me.

DINGER. Too late for me, I'm fucked, beyond that even… but you, if you can, can get this beat…you've plenty of time. Get yourself sorted out…good lookin lass, get yourself a job nay bother, nay bother at all. Good lookin lass like yee…

*(**KERRY** has fallen asleep. **DINGER** doesn't notice.)*

A job in Bede's World. Or the town even. Wearin tights and one of them blazers they wear in the banks, with a name badge that says, Kerry. I can see it. Cos ye never know what can happen.

And I know, I know why the fuck should ye listen to me? I wouldn't listen to me. A fucking stinking old drunk. But you've got to, you've got to try, cus you can't keep on at this…look at the state of me. Do ye want this? You should show these arseholes in here eh. Prove em wrong. Show the fucking lot of them. Whatd'ye say?

*(**KERRY** snores.)*

Aye pet. You show em.

*(**DINGER** sits and stares ahead. There are some quiet snores from **KERRY**. **DINGER** takes the bottle from **KERRY** and sets it on the floor.)*

Come on. Beddy byes.

*(As gently as he can, **DINGER** helps **KERRY** onto the bed and pulls the duvet over her. He gently kisses **KERRY**'s head. He turns and starts to exit but then stops, goes back and picks up the bottle. He stands with it some moments, struggling with what to do. He takes a long drink and sets it back on the floor.)*

Scene Eleven

(The office. **HELEN** *sits at the desk, there is a cup of coffee.* **MIKE** *enters and sits down heavily. He looks terrible.)*

MIKE. Mine?

*(**MIKE** takes the coffee.)*

HELEN. You look like shit.

MIKE. Cheers.

*(**MIKE** takes headache tablets from the filing cabinet and swallows some.)*

Where's Andy?

HELEN. He's left.

MIKE. Where's he gone?

HELEN. He's left here. For good.

MIKE. You're joking. He never said anything to me.

HELEN. No?

MIKE. The little twat. He can't have just left. Where's he left to?

HELEN. Gone home apparently. Rang up yesterday, said it wasn't for him anymore.

MIKE. What, home home? Back to his…

HELEN. Yep.

MIKE. He just…he never said he was…why wouldn't he speak to me?

HELEN. Don't know, maybe he didn't know he needed your permission.

MIKE. It's a bit, it's a bit fucking rude do you not think?

HELEN. Rude?

MIKE. We... I thought we...if he was going to leave I'd have thought he'd have told me.

HELEN. Maybe he wanted a clean break.

MIKE. A clean break. What's that supposed to mean?

HELEN. Bit touchy this morning. How come you're late?

MIKE. They don't fit Peugot's with alarm clocks.

HELEN. Slept in the car, nice.

MIKE. I need to ask a favour Helen.

(Pause.)

It's a bit tricky.

HELEN. Go on.

MIKE. I need somewhere to stay for a bit.

HELEN. You what?

MIKE. I wouldn't ask but...a few nights...

HELEN. God. Has she...? about us?

MIKE. Us?

HELEN. Us, whatever it is/ that we...

MIKE. That. Christ no. That's just fucking. She wouldn't... not like this, over that.

HELEN. Great.

MIKE. A week... I'll sort it. Just a few days while/ I...

HELEN. Sort what?

MIKE. Same old shite, I don't remember, I was fucking shitfaced...just till I can get this sorted out.

Fuck sake Helen, please. You won't even know I'm there. I've nowhere else. I thought Andy but...

HELEN. Andy's gone.

MIKE. So you say. You seem quite pleased by that.

HELEN. The last thing he needs is...

MIKE. The last thing he needs!

HELEN. Don't you think you've caused him enough problems?

MIKE. Anyway, you've got loads of room, please.

(Slight Pause.)

I think she means it this time. She's changed the fucking locks on us.

HELEN. It wouldn't even occur to you.

MIKE. What?

HELEN. No. That I would fucking say no. I'm not going to have you in my house. Jesus. You don't see it do you? What you do to people.

There was a time I'd have helped you without thinking about it. No questions asked. What a fucking idiot.

So what's your plan now then?

MIKE. What?

HELEN. Your plan, for this situation. What's your approach? You're good at this, can't wait to hear it. Andy was plan A. I was next, I'm all ears. Got any one else lined up?

MIKE. Don't be like that, I just need some time Helen, to sort myself out, show her that I can…stop the drink and that.

HELEN. Ha, you honestly think it's that simple?

*(**DINGER** enters. He wears clean clothes and has washed. He is shaking violently and wretched from alcohol withdrawal.)*

HELEN. Jesus, Dinger.

MIKE. Christ.

*(**DINGER** falls.)*

HELEN. You alright Dinger?

*(**HELEN** and **MIKE** get up to help him.)*

DINGER. Stamp.

HELEN. What?

MIKE. Let's get him sat down.

*(**HELEN** and **MIKE** support **DINGER** to a chair at the desk.)*

DINGER. I need… I need…stamp.

MIKE. Have you gone cold turkey?

DINGER. Stamp.

HELEN. How long since you had a drink?

DINGER. Trying to stop...trying to stop...stamp.

MIKE. For fuck sake, you should know better than that.

HELEN. When did you last have a drink?

DINGER. Been cutting down, nothing today...need a stamp.

HELEN. Nothing today, at all!

(MIKE *takes a quarter bottle of vodka from his pocket and puts it in* DINGER's *hands.*)

MIKE. Here, drink that.

HELEN. What the hell are you doing?

DINGER. I need to stop.

MIKE. He'll fucking kill himself stopping like that.

(MIKE *raises the bottle to* DINGER's *mouth and he drinks. This settles him a bit.* MIKE *takes the bottle, pours some into a mug in front of* DINGER *then put the bottle back in his pocket.* DINGER *drinks the contents of the mug.* HELEN *looks at* MIKE.)

MIKE. What?

HELEN. Why Dinger? What's brought this on?

DINGER. I need a stamp...couple of days since...

HELEN. Since what?

DINGER. She wrote to us, out the blue...she's twenty one.

HELEN. Who?

DINGER. Rebecca, my little girl.

(DINGER *produces a birthday card.*)

HELEN. Dinger, that's amazing,

DINGER. Need a stamp for her card.

HELEN. And that's why you're trying to stop?

DINGER. I've got to. I've arranged to see her next week. I couldn't let her see me like that. I need you to help me Helen.

HELEN. Of course I'll help you Dinger.

DINGER. I know you laughed at us before Mike, but I mean it this time.

HELEN. I'll get you seen today Dinger.

DINGER. Thank you. I'm shitting meself. I mean, I don't even know what to say in this. Happy birthday, sorry I've been shit all your life.

HELEN. Happy birthday, love Dad'll probably do.

DINGER. Just after...this time and...what can I say to her? Look at me. I've done nothing for her...fucked off and spent my life...last time she would've seen us I was all cut, had tried to charge through the patio window, carted off by the polis, her crying, blood all over.

(**DINGER** *cries.*)

What can I say?

(**HELEN** *puts her arm around him.*)

Look at the state of me. What can I do for her?

(*Pause.*)

HELEN. She, she won't be expecting you to...

Hey, I never thought I'd be this close to Dinger and not be overcome by the aroma of stale piss.

(**HELEN** *sniffs the air.*)

In fact, unless I'm wildly mistaken. Is is that shampoo I can smell?

DINGER. It certainly is. That's Herbal Essences, enriched with Aloe Vera.

Fuck sake, what's she going to think? I can't go and... not like this...

MIKE. Listen to me, if you don't do this, there won't be a day you won't regret it. Now get your card writ ye daft shite.

(**MIKE** *gets up and puts a pen in front of* **DINGER**.)

DINGER. Right.

(MIKE opens the card on the desk. There are tears in DINGER's eyes. His hand shakes as he writes. HELEN holds the card still and MIKE steadies his arm.)

Dear. Rebecca.

My fucking writing.

Happy birthday.

(Pause.)

Love. Dad.

MIKE. Do a kiss.

DINGER. Kiss. There.

(MIKE puts the card in the envelope while HELEN gets a stamp which she then sticks on the envelope. MIKE is struggling to maintain composure.)

Thank you Helen.

HELEN. Right, come on Dinger. Do you think you can manage anything to eat?

DINGER. I think so.

(HELEN drops the key to room Q on the desk and then helps DINGER up.)

HELEN. *(as she exits with DINGER)* I've done the handover sheet Mike. Room Q's empty.

(HELEN and DINGER exit. MIKE contemplates this. Fade to black.)

(The end.)